THRIVING AS A
PROFESSIONAL TEACHL

Thriving as a Professional Teacher explores the tensions and balance between developing the classroom you know will be best for the children you teach, and facing external pressures such as Ofsted, performance management, Teacher Standards and the need to prepare children for SATs and other tests.

The book locates the professional in the political context before outlining the key challenges faced and experienced, and laying the foundations necessary for the professional to thrive. An expert team of contributors analyses the differences between professionalism and 'professionalisation', and emphasises the importance of promoting a collaborative, sharing culture to give you the knowledge needed to challenge and contest competing agendas. Topics covered include:

- understanding the impact of policy upon teachers and the teaching profession;
- developing a professional identity as a teacher;
- building resilience and a sense of wellbeing as a teacher;
- building and sustaining creativity in the curriculum;
- safeguarding young people;
- examining the impact of globalisation on educational practices.

With case studies, opportunities for reflection and clear chapter summaries woven throughout, *Thriving as a Professional Teacher* will help you to form a sustainable identity and to create a teaching and learning environment in which both teachers and students can thrive. It is an essential read for both trainee and practising teachers.

Ian Luke is Dean of the Faculty of Education, Enterprise and Culture, and University Director for Learning and Teaching at Plymouth Marjon University, UK.

Jan Gourd is Programme Area Lead for Education at Plymouth Marjon University, UK.

THRIVING AS A PROFESSIONAL TEACHER

How to be a Principled Professional

Edited by Ian Luke and Jan Gourd

Routledge
Taylor & Francis Group

LONDON AND NEW YORK

First published 2018
by Routledge
2 Park Square, Milton Park, Abingdon, Oxon OX14 4RN

and by Routledge
711 Third Avenue, New York, NY 10017

Routledge is an imprint of the Taylor & Francis Group, an informa business

British Library Cataloguing in Publication Data
A catalogue record for this book is available from the British Library

Library of Congress Cataloging in Publication Data
Names: Luke, Ian, editor. | Gourd, Jan, editor.
Title: Thriving as a professional teacher : how to be a
principled professional / edited by Ian Luke & Jan Gourd.
Description: Abingdon, Oxon : New York, NY : Routledge, 2018. |
Includes bibliographical references.
Identifiers: LCCN 2017059170 (print) | LCCN 2018013493 (ebook) |
ISBN 9781138636088 (hbk) | ISBN 9781138636095 (pbk) |
ISBN 9781315206219 (ebk)
Subjects: LCSH: Teachers-Professional relationships. |
Teachers-Work load. | Reflective teaching.
Classification: LCC LB1775 (ebook) | LCC LB1775 .T46 2018 (print) |
DDC 371.102-dc23
LC record available at https://lccn.loc.gov/2017059170

ISBN: 978-1-138-63608-8 (hbk)
ISBN: 978-1-138-63609-5 (pbk)
ISBN: 978-1-315-20621-9 (ebk)

Typeset in Interstate
by Out of House Publishing

MIX
Paper from
responsible sources
FSC   FSC® C013056
www.fsc.org

Printed and bound in Great Britain by
TJ International Ltd, Padstow, Cornwall

Ian Luke: In memory of my mother, Elizabeth 'Joyce' Luke, who was my first and best teacher.

Jan Gourd: In memory of my father, Jim Griffiths, who always liked to try to work hard and enjoy life.

CONTENTS

FIGURES

TABLES

ABOUT THE EDITORS

Ian Luke is Dean of the Faculty of Education, Enterprise and Culture at Plymouth Marjon University. Ian has worked in schools and universities across the UK and has also taught internationally. His research interests include metacognition, professional development, higher education and teacher education. Ian has a strong sporting background in sports acrobatics, winning both world and European medals. He lives with his wife Sophie and their five children in Tavistock, Devon.

Jan Gourd is Programme Area Lead for Education at Plymouth Marjon University. Prior to taking up this post she worked as a primary school head teacher. Jan has taught every year group from EYFS through to Year 6 and has a particular interest in how policy agendas influence pedagogy.

NOTES ON CONTRIBUTORS

Hazel Bending is a Programme Lead for Psychology at Plymouth Marjon University. She has worked in higher education for a number of years, teaching students on Psychology, SEN, Education and Health programmes. Hazel has keen interest in supporting professional development and wellbeing.

Anne Bradley is a lecturer in Primary ITT at Plymouth Marjon University. Her specialist areas are Primary English and History and her research interests are focused on enabling children to have access to high-quality reading texts. Prior to her current role she has worked in primary schools for more than 20 years, teaching in Key Stages 1 and 2, as English subject leader and senior manager. She currently works with trainee teachers supporting their development in the role of classroom practitioner and enabling them to understand the pedagogy behind this role.

MarkAndrew Dearden is a senior lecturer within the education team at Plymouth Marjon University. Prior to taking up this post he worked as a primary school head teacher. MarkAndrew has taught all year groups from reception through to Year 6 and has particular interests in the curriculum subjects Art and Design and Religious Education, and with the development of curriculum design and school ethos in changing times.

Sally Eales is a senior lecturer in primary education at the Plymouth Marjon University, particularly supporting students in the first year of the BEd Primary programmes. Before working in Initial Teacher Education (ITE) she taught in a range of primary schools across Devon and has senior leadership and advisory teacher experience. Sally works across a range of ITE programmes with a particular focus on school partnerships and supporting the mentoring of trainees in schools. Her other key interests are primary literacy and professional studies.

Gill Golder is Director of Teacher Education and Department Head for Education at Plymouth Marjon University. She has 13 years of experience teaching 11-18 age range in a range of comprehensive schools holding middle and senior leadership positions. Having made the move to higher education she has been recognised for excellence in teaching and learning on a range of undergraduate and postgraduate programmes. Her research interests lie in organisational structure and processes and the triumvirate relationship between policy, practice and research.

Suzanne Hope is a lecturer in primary education. She has taught in the UK and overseas. Her primary interests are engaging children in dialogic approaches such as drama, discussion and critical literacy.

Sean MacBlain currently works at Plymouth Marjon University; he previously worked as a Senior Lecturer in Education and Developmental Psychology at Stranmillis University College, a College of Queens University Belfast. Sean also worked for many years as a teacher and then an educational psychologist. Sean's research interests include the professional development of teachers and early years practitioners and the social and emotional development of children and young people with special educational needs and disabilities.

Alison Milner currently works at South Devon College. Alison is the programme coordinator for HE, Child Development & Education; overseeing the early years and teaching provision in HE as well as the ITE courses for the whole college. She teaches on various programmes within her area, working with students and staff in developing their knowledge and skills in education for all ages. Alison's research interests are around the nature of identity for the professional touching on values and motivations within practice.

Tanya Ovenden-Hope PFHEA is Professor of Education at Plymouth Marjon University and has more than 27 years' experience in teaching, teacher education and educational leadership. An innovative academic, Tanya's research is on educational improvement and effectiveness, with a focus on educational isolation and challenges for schools. Her commitment to championing the importance of, and developing new ways of thinking about, learning and teaching was recognised when she was awarded Principal Fellow of the Higher Education Academy in 2014 and the National Enterprise Educator Award in 2014.

Chris Simpson is a senior lecturer at Plymouth Marjon University, leading foundation programmes in education and in early years. She has many years' practice experience in education and a particular interest in life-long learning.

Sue Wayman is a senior lecturer at Plymouth Marjon University. Sue's academic interests relate to global education, education for sustainability and practitioner research. Her doctorate involved methodological development in poststructural discourse analysis. Sue has also completed research and evaluation of religious education linked to DfE funding, and within informal educational contexts.

ACKNOWLEDGEMENTS

The editors would like to thank and acknowledge Ivor Goodson.

Ivor's work with regards to professional knowledge, professional lives and principled professionalism formed the foundation for this book. His work and insight are both implicitly and explicitly embedded within every chapter.

Introduction

Ian Luke and Jan Gourd

Goodson's (2003) notion of *principled professionalism* suggests that professionalism should hold cognitive and emotional dimensions of learning and teaching within a firm understanding of the moral and social purposes of education. However, in the current educational climate it would appear that this notion of professionalism is being challenged. As it is noted in Chapter 1, there is a discomfort with how education is being seen as a commodity (Moss, 2015) bound by the logics of 'marketisation, competition and cost-benefit analysis' (Apple, 2013, p. 6). Such philosophical drivers have meant that teachers are now faced with a clear performativity agenda and high stakes accountability. There is a *regulatory gaze* that emanates from the performativity agenda (Osgood, 2006, p. 7) that is having an impact on the behaviour of schools, leaders, teachers, parents and pupils.

Sachs (2001, p. 151) suggests that there is an emerging *managerial professionalism* imposed in the guise of governmental education policy; one that, 'gains its legitimacy through the promulgation of policies and the allocation of funds associated with those policies'. Ryan and Bourke (2013, p. 421) bluntly state that policy is attempting to shape teaching, 'through behavioural-heavy standards, with little regard for the attitudinal, emotional and intellectual dimensions of the trustworthy professional'.

This new form of professionalism seeks to ensure quality through techno-rational processes that are akin to the manufacturing industry whereby *quality control* can *tick off* a number of standards that the product should meet. This kind of professional is often said to be constructed through techno-rationalism which is linked to a neoliberal ideology. In neoliberal ideology a dominant theme is value for money. In terms of teacher education, if a trainee teacher can meet a number of pre-determined standards then they have developed into a *quality* teacher, a product that was worth the investment and is value for money. This teacher in turn can teach a curriculum that ensures that the teaching they provide is value for money in terms of the children's learning. Education and economics are not far apart in political discourse (MacBlain, Dunn & Luke, 2017). This teaching is checked by the testing regime that children are subjected to from a very young age.

The customer (usually in this case the parent), it is purported, can choose the best-quality school for their child based on the published outcomes of the tests the children have taken. Compliance with the curriculum and certain teaching methods is ensured by an inspection, the results of which are published and also carry penalties or sanctions for those found not to be fully compliant with current legislation.

Goodson (2003, p. 132) argues that principled professionalism, with its moral purpose, must challenge such narrow views of *professionalisation*. *Active care* should replace *service* to students, a *collaborative culture* should be encouraged, and *continuous learning* should replace *compliance*.

Education is a transformative experience and students should be provided with opportunities, within a supportive environment, to develop greater understanding of their potential, their role and their impact within a wider community. Moss (2015) asks us to consider Facer's (2011, p.15) vision where educational environments have a role of *future building*, allowing individuals and communities to, 'contest the visions of the future that they are being presented with… to fight for viable futures for all'. The result could be individual and community aspiration, resilience, creativity and wellbeing; enhanced public understanding and *voice*, and enhanced individual and community productivity. As such, this book will examine various issues using the moral and social purposes of education as a foundation, and consider how individuals and communities can benefit from approaching education within a more *principled professionalism* framework.

This book came about from our concern over the increasing number of teachers leaving the teaching profession within the first five years of their careers (Roffey, 2012; Savage 2017). The House of Commons Education Committee (2017, p. 2) argues, 'the Government should place greater emphasis on improving teacher retention' and acknowledges the impact of the changes to the school system and accountability in increasing workload for teachers. Teachers need to be sustained (Downey, Schaefer & Clandinin, 2014) and they need to thrive. As academics who are involved with the education and training of future teachers, this attrition rate is of immediate concern. How can we prepare future teachers better to cope with the pressures that teaching and a life in school brings? How can we develop resilience within our new teachers so that they are able to become mature experienced principled professionals rather than feeling they need to leave so early in their chosen career?

In discussion, we found that many of the students and early career teachers that we engaged with talked to us informally about their frustrations of working in a performativity-driven system. A system that is driven by a neoliberal ideology of measurement and seeking to prove value for money. The performativity agenda is challenging professional autonomy. As soon as these new teachers go into their first jobs they can see that the relational aspects of their jobs, the concern they have for their pupils' wellbeing, is often marginalised, under-valued, because it is not *measurable*. Yet it is those relational and values-based skills that make the difference between an *average* teacher and a teacher who adds real value to their pupils' lives and life chances.

It is the principled professional, the inspirational, motivational, caring and loving teacher who makes the difference, who is the teacher who has the chance of narrowing the gap between the educationally disadvantaged and the educationally privileged (Noddings, 2013). Teachers who have a strong values-based pedagogy, who demonstrate *principled professionalism* are the teachers who often find fulfilment working in more challenging schools in difficult socio-economic neighbourhoods. Those schools, however, are often likely to be the most harshly judged as their data are hard-won and often viewed to be 'not good enough'. This leads to such schools losing their teachers at an even faster rate (Staufenberg, 2017). This book is an attempt to analyse the stressors and the protectors within the lives of both teachers and the pupils in their care. We seek to show readers how to consider and critically reflect on the issues in order to potentially increase their resilience while not losing their *soul* as Ball (2003) alludes to.

In essence, how can teachers develop into principled professionals (Goodson, 2003) and how can we help them to achieve this without diminishing their motivation, the motivation that drew them to seek a teaching career in the first place?

Venning, Wilson, Kettler and Eliott (2012), in their study of adolescent mental health, categorise individuals as flourishing, languishing, struggling or floundering. Our hope here is to promote flourishing as the ideal state in which teachers operate. This book is an attempt to help aspiring and new teachers to think through the issues they encounter in a critically reflective way that develops their activism and sense of control over their situation. In that way we hope to help them to flourish and thrive (Seligman, Ernst, Gillham, Reivich & Linkins, 2009; Seligman 2012) and it is our belief that principled professionals who are thriving can indeed bring about flourishing and achievement in their pupils.

The book is separated into three sections. Part I, 'Locating the professional in the political context', focuses on the importance of recognising the political influences on education. Each author identifies how important it is to sustain a *professional identity* and for teachers to promote a collaborative, sharing culture. Part II, 'Challenges facing the professional', sees the authors wrestling with issues that will impact upon the ability of the professional teacher to thrive. Finally, Part III 'Laying the foundations for the thriving professional' deliberates the building blocks for the professional teacher; in particular the importance of principles, resilience and wellbeing for the professional teacher. The final chapter in the section pulls the key themes of the whole book together, discussing the significance of *reflective practice* in forming a strong, sustainable professional identity and forming the basis for a collaborative teaching and learning environment in which teachers and pupils can thrive. As such, every chapter within this book explores dominant issues teachers encounter. Each chapter contains several 'Pause to reflect' boxes; we hope that you will try to do these activities as you are reading as they may help you place the theory in context to your own understanding and principled practice.

References

Apple, M.W. (2013) *Can Education Change Society?* Abingdon: Routledge.

Ball, S.J. (2003) The teacher's soul and the terrors of performativity. *Journal of Education Policy*, 18(1), 215-228.

Downey, C.A., Schaefer, L. & Clandinin, D.J. (2014) Shifting teacher education from 'skilling up' to sustaining beginning teachers. *Learning Landscapes*, 8(1), 15-20.

Facer, K. (2011) *Learning Futures: Education, Technology and Social Change.* London: Routledge.

Goodson, I. (2000) The principled professional. *Prospects*, 30(2), 182-188.

Goodson, I. (2003) *Professional Knowledge, Professional Lives: Studies in Education and Change.* Maidenhead: Open University Press.

House of Commons Education Committee (2017) *Recruitment and Retention of Teachers: Fifth Report of Session 2016-2017.* House of Commons. Available at https://publications.parliament.uk/pa/cm201617/cmselect/cmeduc/199/199.pdf.

MacBlain, S., Dunn, J. & Luke, I. (2017) *Contemporary Childhood.* London: Sage.

Moss, P. (2015) There are alternatives! Contestation and hope in early childhood education. *Global Studies of Childhood*, 5(3), 226-238.

Noddings, N. (2013) *Caring: A Feminine Approach to Ethics and Moral Education.* Berkeley, CA: University of California Press.

Osgood, J. (2006) Deconstructing professionalism in early childhood education: resisting the regulatory gaze. *Contemporary Issues in Early Childhood*, 7(1), 5-14.

Roffey, S. (2012) Pupil wellbeing - teacher wellbeing: two sides of the same coin? *Educational & Child Psychology*, 29(4), 8-17.

Ryan, M. & Bourke, T. (2013) The teacher as reflexive professional: making visible the excluded discourse in teacher standards. *Discourse: Studies in the Cultural Politics of Education*, 34(3), 411-423.

Sachs, J. (2001) Teacher professional identity: competing discourses, competing outcomes. *Journal of Educational Policy*, 16(2), 149-161.

Savage, M. (2017) Almost a quarter of teachers who have qualified since 2011 have left profession. *The Guardian*, 8 July 2017. Available at www.theguardian.com/education/2017/jul/08/almost-a-quarter-of-teachers-who-have-qualified-since-2011-have-left-profession.

Seligman, M.E.P. (2012) *Flourish:A Visionary New Understanding of Happiness and Well-Being*. New York: Free Press.

Seligman, M.E.P., Ernst, R.M., Gillham, J., Reivich, K. & Linkins, M. (2009) Positive education: positive psychology and classroom interventions. *Oxford Review of Education*, 35(3), 293–231.

Staufenberg, J. (2017) Teachers 70% more likely to leave schools in poorer areas. *Schools Week*, 13 July 2017. Available at https://schoolsweek.co.uk/teachers-70-more-likely-to-leave-schools-in-poorer-areas-new-report-shows/.

Venning, A., Wilson, A., Kettler, L. & Eliott, J.A. (2012) Mental health among youth in South Australia: a survey of flourishing, languishing, struggling and floundering. *Australian Psychologist*, 48, 299–310.

PART I

Locating the professional in the political context

1 Policy, professionals and professionalism

Ian Luke, Tanya Ovenden-Hope and Alison Milner

Introduction

This chapter will explore the implications of policy upon teachers and their practice. Once policy is established it is, 'intimately and deliberatively woven' into the fabric of practice (Lea, 2013, p. 21). Policy will regulate content, curriculum, pedagogy and, therefore teachers. Through identifying political *drivers*, the intentions and ideology behind policy, it becomes clear that there is need for teachers to explicitly consider how they *position* themselves; they can either be positioned by policy or position themselves within policy (Lea, 2013). There are *algorithms of accountability* that put pressure on individuals and education communities alike (MacBlain, Dunn & Luke, 2017, p. 150) and it is imperative, therefore, that teachers are able to appreciate what is negotiable and what is non-negotiable within their own professional identity, but also for these teachers to be supported and *sustained* (Downey, Schaefer & Clandinin, 2014) in a collaborative culture such as a Professional Learning Community (PLC) (Owen, 2016).

> **By the end of the chapter you will:**
> - Develop an understanding of how policy and political discourse can have an impact upon practice and practitioners.
> - Understand the need for educationalists to have a deep understanding of their own professional values and identity.
> - Understand the importance of, but also difficulties in, developing a collaborative culture and Professional Learning Communities.

Contemporary political ideology

There is no doubting that education has gained significant attention in recent years. In principle, being viewed as *high priority* can lead to recognition, support and additional resources, but the implications of being *high priority* depend heavily upon the underpinning ideological drivers. With that, we need to be mindful of how Campbell-Barr and Leeson (2016) suggest that *reasoning* behind policies and regulation can often be *hidden*, which obviously is a worrying scenario in education if the reasoning and underpinning principles are not in alignment with the values and principles of teachers.

Notably, Moss (2015) highlights his discomfort with how education is being treated as a commodity, bound by the logics of, 'marketisation, competition and cost-benefit analysis' (Apple, 2013, p. 6). Such neoliberal philosophical drivers have meant that teachers are now faced with a clear performativity agenda with high-stakes accountability. Parents, schools, teachers and pupils are drawn into a performativity agenda that can undermine the essence and aims of education. Goodson's (2000, 2003) notion of *principled professionalism* that holds cognitive and emotional dimensions of learning and teaching within a firm understanding of the moral and social purposes of education, is being squeezed by political drivers that focus on outcome and perceived *quality* without taking into account context, values, subjectivity and plurality (Moss & Dahlberg, 2008).

Performativity

Ball (2003, p. 216) defines performativity as 'a technology, a culture and a mode of regulation that employs judgements, comparisons and displays as means of control, attrition and change – based on rewards and sanctions (both material and symbolic)'.

Wilkins (2010) notes that performative systems are characterised by three key strands of policy and practice. First, there is the use of audit or target data, which can potentially lead to risk-averse practice and the suppression of professional dialogue. It would appear axiomatic that targets drive behaviours, but this also means they can sometimes drive the wrong types of behaviour. An outcome-focused pedagogy can emerge (Ryan & Bourke, 2013) for example, as outputs are pushed to the foreground (Loh, 2013). It is possible that, 'commitment, judgement and authenticity within practice are sacrificed for impression and performance' (Ball, 2004, p. 146). Turner-Bisset (2007, p. 195, cited in Loh, 2013) confirms this, noting, 'teachers compromise on the kinds of teaching in which they believe, and [enact] the kinds of teaching demanded by performativity'.

Second, there is the use of interventionist regulatory mechanisms, often high-stakes, with regular monitoring and inspection. Of course, high-stakes *accountability* is very different to high-stakes *responsibility*. Teachers should be responsible for their actions and the impact they are having upon children's learning. However, this is different to feeling they have accountability but without control or autonomy. Far from driving *standards* of education forward, the implications of high stakes accountability mean innovative and creative teaching practices become squeezed, children's experiences are narrowed and the very professional identity of teachers is threatened. The disconcerting irony is that high-stakes accountability clashes with what is hoped to be achieved. Take, for example, the current political drive for STEM education; the experiences and love of these subjects cannot easily be nurtured in early childhood due to the need for schools and teachers to focus on a narrow range of subjects that the school will be held accountable for nearing the end of primary education. Adams, Monahan and Wills (2015) have already highlighted how this threatens the more holistic education of a child. Of course, there are other consequences. Crocco and Costigan (2007, cited in Olivant, 2015) argue, for example, that struggling with high-stakes accountability without a sense of control or autonomy has particularly troubling implications for economically disadvantaged schools with higher percentages of *at-risk* students. They argue that while some teachers can be resilient to these pressures, others find these conditions too stressful and are leaving underperforming schools for settings where stakes are not so high in terms of student *failure* on standardised tests.

Pause to reflect

Consider four quadrants: high-stakes accountability, low-stakes accountability, high-stakes responsibility and, finally, low-stakes responsibility. Which of these situations do you feel would best optimise teacher effectiveness? What is the basis for your answer?

Third, performance systems are based within a *market* environment that enables the process of audit and inspection to reinforce the power of disciplinary actions; as Wilkins (2010, p. 398) states, 'market levers are crucial to the neo-liberal model of governance'. Loh (2013) notes that schools as organisations are subject to these performativity pressures; relationships with parents have fundamentally changed, for example, with education being viewed as an exchange of services and goods. Parents have made an *investment* and are free to choose the schools they put their children in. As a result, schools try to stand out and seek to market themselves as *value added* (Loh, 2013, p. 163).

Professionalism

Wilkins (2010) also noted the impact, the potentially disempowering impact, between the demands of the performativity agenda and notions of professional autonomy. The *regulatory gaze* that emanates from the performativity agenda, can inevitably lead teachers to 'conform to dominant constructions of professionalism' (Osgood, 2006, p. 7). Ryan and Bourke (2013) also argue there is a move towards *performative professionalism* (Beck, 2008), where teachers are expected to demonstrate or perform so to enable the profession to be monitored and *visible*. The fear, as noted by Wilkins (2010, p. 393) is that, 'political and public pressure for accountability has led to concern that teachers have become increasingly de-professionalised and compliant in the delivery of state-imposed initiatives'. Indeed, Loh (2013) notes performativity could require a potential sacrifice of professionalism for accountability and refers to Ball (2004) in defining a 'post professional'; a teacher who can, 'adapt to the necessities and vicissitudes of policy' (p. 17) and who can 'set aside personal beliefs and commitments and live an existence of calculation' (Ball, 2003, p. 215). Beck (2008) attests to this, suggesting that such neo-liberal policies can actually use the *mask* of re-professionalisation while initiating a process of de-professionalisation.

Pause to reflect

Evans (2008, p. 32-33) wrestles with the difficulties of defining professionalism, but suggests it may be useful to distinguish between professionalism that is *demanded* or *requested* (e.g., professional service level demands), professionalism that is *prescribed* (e.g., recommended professional service levels perceived by analysts) and professionalism that is *enacted* (e.g., professional practice as observed, perceived or interpreted from outside or within the professional group).

What are the differences in demanded, prescribed and enacted professionalism within teaching?

Finding a new professionalism

In order to challenge this scenario and an enforced *performative* or *post* view of professionalism, two key themes emerge. First, teachers need to position themselves to mediate the impact of political discourse on themselves and their identity (Lea, 2013) and second, there is a need to resist and counter political forces through collegiality and collectivism (Sachs, 2003).

Position in policy and professional identity

Notably, Meyerson (2004) used the term 'tempered radical' for those individuals who, because they understood the fact that organisations were continually evolving, were able to balance the need to be seen as *corporate* with the need to challenge and change. The implication is that such tempered radicals take advantage of opportunities to challenge, push boundaries, because they are explicitly aware of what is negotiable for them as individuals, and what is simply non-negotiable. Carlone, Haun-Frank and Kimmel (2010, p. 941) similarly noted how teachers worked as tempered radicals, 'working the system' as they struggled with the 'many biases, contradictions and unintended consequences' of education policy. It is suggested that such an approach can provide a clarity, strength, resilience and confidence in teachers enabling them maintain a sense of identity they are comfortable with and enabling them to thrive (MacBlain et al., 2017).

It is implied that those who embrace or simply fail to position themselves within the political discourse could become 'tick-box professionals who present a veneer of quality' (Ryan & Bourke, 2013, p. 421). It is worth noting that Wilkins' small-scale study of newly qualified primary teachers showed signs of an emerging *post-performative* professionalism, where teachers, 'fully embrace the accountability culture of teaching, less from a sense of democratic duty as public servants than simply because it is *effective*' (Wilkins, 2010, p. 405, emphasis in original). Wilkins continued:

> they have little patience for those amongst their experienced colleagues who they see as resistant to change, and are generally comfortable with the wider framework of performative management cultures – so long as they continue to enjoy the 'micro-autonomy' of the classroom.
>
> (Wilkins, 2010, p. 405)

It has been argued that teachers have 'restricted teacher professional identities' due to the pressures of neoliberal subjectivities (Hall & McGinity, 2015, p. 2), which may help explain Wilkins' (2010) findings. Nevertheless, there is the question whether such *resilience* would remain longer-term, and more importantly, how can resilience and wellbeing be optimised.

Downey et al. (2014) argue that it is too easy for early career teachers to lose resilience and it is imperative that they are encouraged to focus on *sustaining moments* as it is these moments, 'that can turn into stories that will sustain them in teaching' (Schaefer & Clandinin, 2011, p. 291). For Downey et al. (2014, p. 17), 'the process of becoming a teacher is a means to live out who they are, and are becoming, not an end in and of itself' and 'becoming a particular kind of teacher was interwoven with becoming a particular kind of person'. As such, rather than assuming professionalism and professional development is about 'skilling up' to cope with issues of resilience and retention we should be attending to what *sustains* teachers. In their view, this will require reflective *spaces* where teachers can, 'turn back upon the stories that brought them to becoming teachers' (Schaefer & Clandinin, 2011, p. 293). In succinct terms Korthagen (2017) noted that while it may be an 'inconvenient truth' for policymakers, 'the connection with the person of the teacher is crucial' (p. 387), and as such, it is imperative that we examine this balance of personal and professional identity and how we can support and sustain teachers. We cannot hide from the fact that the National Union of Teachers (2017) reported that 45 per cent of young teachers have concerns over their mental health and are considering leaving the profession. Teachers need sustaining.

The Buffer-fly (Milner, 2017) is a useful concept to examine the balance and influences of these personal and professional identities, and how it is possible for a professional to thrive.

The Buffer-fly

The nature of identity from a professional teaching perspective, can be complex and confusing. The dualism of personal and professional identity provides distinctive elements to be considered when addressing the context of the role and the responsibilities for a position. The perceived separateness of identity when acting, behaving or being professional is sometimes so removed from the concept of personal identity that the positionality of the two are poles apart. Problems can arise in the uniting of personal and professional identity with consideration being made for the possible outcomes and their disconnected nature. Harmony of personal and professional identity can be linked when amalgamating goals, aspirations and intended action for the academic (Billett & Pavlova, 2005). However, the imbalance of the two aspects of identity can also necessitate disillusionment with the roles and responsibilities of the teacher when there are deep-seated differences in the goals, aspirations and actions.

One way that this can be overcome is through the utilisation of the Buffer-fly concept whereby the nature of identity can be positioned as such to establish boundaries and similarities for the individual in their role and personal identity. The crossover of the two entwined aspects of identity can be understood by the deriving the amount of crossover. Determining the key factors identified in both personal and professional identity will enable the pattern to be created to support the alignment the academic has with their given role from a personal as well as professional perspective.

Identification of individual values such as power, beliefs, conformity, selfhood, acceptance and trust will provide a basis on which to determine the individual's natural alignment to the political motivations of the role professionally with the individual values fostered prior to entering the position.

To begin with the two main themes resonating from the Buffer-fly, the political alignment and individual values. For the purposes of this concept, political alignment outlines the determinate factors related to the educational setting or establishment, the sector and the motivations of governance from policy. The political aspects of alignment promote and at the same time prohibit the establishment of change for the individual, setting and/or sector. With this in mind, consideration of factors that are outside of the individual's control have a bearing on the arena of educational transformation. Whether this is positive or negative will ultimately be determined by the individual within their role, adoption of the responsibilities and the boundaries accorded by wider internal as well as external policy.

As with any concept, defining key aspects of the individual distinctiveness is not clear-cut; the Buffer-fly provides a rationale regarding the relationship between the personal and professional identity of each academic teacher. The six identified integral aspects of the individual for establishing the identity of the academic are:

- Beliefs
- Acceptance – being and belonging
- Selfhood
- Trust
- Power
- Conformity.

Beliefs are determined as a result of our individual upbringing (Lee and Schallert, 2016). They are informed by people around us, through family units, communities and influential individuals in our lives. The identity that we ultimately configure is inextricably linked with our own experience of life as we grow and develop from children into adults. Values and beliefs develop and grow, providing changes with our fledgling experience, the experiential element of learning supports the construct of our own individual beliefs. The impact that our beliefs have on own identity formation create tensions that fluctuate depending on the experience at the time (Beijaard, Meijer & Verloop, 2004). The results are that the individual acts and behaves according to their beliefs, creating an identity uniting both professional and personal identity. However, the discord with a series of belief and values that are not entirely accepted within the professional role can and will foster disharmony. The unity of professional and personal beliefs is fundamental in providing academics (teachers) with the means to maintain equilibrium of self in the acceptance of their role.

Acceptance, being and belonging, in any aspect of life, acknowledges the arrival of the individual. When aligned to the role of the professional academic teacher, the need to belong, especially in a Western perspective, can be linked to Maslow's hierarchy of needs (1954). The academic teacher can draw their own narrative in understanding and linking the responsibilities to their own professional role. The exploration to uncover the depth of recognition for the role will lead the individual academic to sketch their own meaning and acceptance.

Understanding the nuances of a given role provides a sense of knowing and privilege apportioned to the confident and able professionals (Lewis, 2014). The balance between the socially acceptable and the individual acceptance of agency supports the actions and deliberate choices made to improve self and develop beyond the perceptions of own goals. Acceptance within the constructs of the Buffer-fly supports the notion of growth for the individual to develop a sense of self, enhancing being in the moment and becoming through the transition of growth in confidence, ability and knowledge to be.

Selfhood combined with the empowerment of role, responsibilities and professional identity also extends to the acceptance of unpredictability (Vass, 2015). The idea that the clear boundaries of a role and the development of knowledge are tantamount to the continued exploration of agency and self evolve with the growth of the professional. However, what is not always explicit is the stability of the role and/or the responsibilities likewise associated with the job description. Selfhood, by definition, however, is the construct of internalised narrative (Hökkä, Vähäsantanen & Mahlakaarto, 2017). The ability to modify and reconstruct presents a potential conflict in the knowing and being of self, whether professional or personal. The identified conflict is that in the very being and becoming of self and/or attaining selfhood means that their journey is incomplete. When entwined with the flourishing of the Buffer-fly, the ability to negotiate and change when required is imperative to move with the times and the arena that is education. While the beliefs and values of the individual will not alter, there is an ability to flow with the process and work within the boundaries of change, acknowledging the movement but not fighting self in the modification of the ideal. The momentum through the passage of change is to flourish and evolve with strength and resilience creating a great self and identity.

The power that is accrued through the development of self is one that is gathered through the various experiences that have presented themselves during an individual's life. Although harrowing experiences can be damaging for the individual, the experience can also be the catalyst to power and control - creating a self-assured professional who is able to weather the storm and transform as and when required (Mansfield, Beltman, Broadley & Weatherby-Fell, 2016). The Buffer-fly allows the development of power to be semiotic, through language and behaviour the individual is able to fully actualise through self-belief. This is not to say that the professional through the transformation is a conceited self-serving individual but one who is able to empathise with those around, developing a lens though which external perspectives can be viewed and valued for what they are (Pajak, 2012). Power can also be the driving force in the quest for quality in practice and in structure and systems (Lukes, 2004). Self-image is subsequently enhanced through efficacy and satisfaction when measuring in relation to roles and responsibilities professionally and personally.

Trust, which is not always given the due that it deserves, is essential in the maintenance of self and promoting a sense of worth and being, both personally and professionally (Lount, 2010). The notion of community fostering values and beliefs supports the individual in trusting themselves and also others. The network and connections that are generated through shared beliefs and values are powerful, uniting individuals in a common goal and or project. Through the respect of peers and the recognition of a 'good job', approach and or attitude to learning, trust can be earnt. Trust can take time to nurture, it is a commodity that is built on and established through professional and personal relationships. The forming of collective identities when professionals are working together, and are united by the aims and objectives of their own professionalism, allow for the growth of a cultural identity within these workplaces.

The exclusive nature of conformity is such that the individuals understand the boundaries and support in place to aid the development of self but also through the collective identities created through a culture of learning. Conformity and developing a shared knowledge of known information promotes the communal identity (Lukes, 2004). The notion of conformity secures the boundaries that unite and divide individuals, constructing frameworks in which to adhere and respect the individuals within. While this is an acknowledgement of the positive aspects of community working, communities select those who are keepers and those who are not (Becker, 1963). This distinction, although potentially damaging to some individuals, further ensures the community in which the individual is establishing themselves professionally is conforming to a set of norms and values that whether explicit or not promote engagement of individuals who are willing to support each other. The flourishing of the Buffer-fly empowers individuals to conform to the norms of a set professional identity, ensuring there are ground rules and established boundaries for interaction to be endorsed.

Although individually the composite parts of the Buffer-fly are unique and necessary for the individual to thrive, Milner (2017) argues it is only when the six composite components of the 'thorax' at the centre are recognised in equal proportions that the growth and transformation of the individual can begin. The composite parts of the Buffer-fly also lay foundations for effective collaborative cultures and teachers' engagement within such cultures.

Collegiality and collaboration: Professional Learning Communities (PLCs)

Osgood (2010, p. 119) argues that political discourse is so dominant that it can effectively silence alternative debates around professionalism and what it means to be professional, and posits that educators must define professionalism from within. Aligned with these thoughts, Goodson (2003, p.132) argued that we need to develop a perspective around professionalism that encourages a collaborative culture and replaces compliance with continuous learning. However, establishing a collaborative culture is no easy task, especially when performativity threatens the very notion of *social connections* (Olivant, 2015). Indeed, Olivant (2015, p.127) states:

> teachers experience 'fit' with their teaching philosophies and styles and develop social and intellectual connections under conditions that encourage autonomy and teacher professionalism, and thus allow them to foster creativity in the classroom, but experience lack of 'fit' and damaged or broken connections under the current high-stakes testing conditions.

Obviously, therefore, there has been much debate on how best to develop collaborative cultures, and, specifically, the development of Professional Learning Communities (PLCs) and Communities of Practice (CoPs). Wrestling with the theoretical underpinning of establishing collaborative cultures is imperative if we are to gain a clearer picture of what professionalism is, but also because 'successful provision that ensures that all learners progress and achieve, both in academic and wider outcomes, requires a culture of collaboration within and between staff' (Ovenden-Hope & Blandford, 2018, p.23).

There are complications. Blankenship and Ruona (2007) argued, for example, that PLC models are often unclear in how group knowledge can become organisational knowledge and thus adopted throughout the institution; while organisational structures are discussed, there is no reference to the value of social and/or professional networks in knowledge-sharing.

Thus, realising the need for insights into the features of effective PLCs, Owen (2016) reported finding key PLC characteristics for effective teacher learning practices and teacher wellbeing. Arguing that *many* PLCs are 'seemingly only early stage PLCs at best', Owen (2016, p. 2) suggests that they go through a number of stages before they reach the point that they are 'mature' and focused on 'genuine collaboration, joint problem-solving, debate constructive observation and feedback, and support for collegial learning' (p. 4). Owen argues that it is this supportive environment of working with colleagues that addresses issues related to teacher isolation, boredom and burnout due to lack of autonomy and support.

Owen's (2016) case-study research drew on positive psychology for the data analysis framework, and explored the themes of teacher wellbeing, *flourishing* and building resilience through strong relationships. The findings suggest that PLCs have five key characteristics: shared vision and pleasure; trusting relationships and meaning; practical activities and accomplishment; supportive leadership and positive emotion; and collaborative inquiry and learning engagement.

Owen (2016) establishes that the role of school leaders was particularly evident in setting expectations, providing practical support for the PLC and developing a supportive school professional learning culture, and that this explicit support encouraged teachers to be open to trying new classroom practices. In turn, teachers reported in their interviews that the work undertaken in PLCs significantly improved student learning and that this gave them 'a real sense of accomplishment and meaning for their work'; many teachers reported that this would not have happened without a 'highly functioning PLC' (p.14). Following the work of Roffey (2012), Owen provides a model for PLCs in which collegiate relationships foster belonging and a sense of identity: as teachers work together, their individual strengths are valued; as teachers inquire and risk-take together, so their sense of wellbeing, accomplishment and purpose as teachers is enhanced. Owen's (2016) contribution to the debate is to point out that PLCs need to be operating at a mature level for these effects to become apparent. She argues that it is essential that PLCs move beyond conviviality, and that they build a sense of identity and purpose with members genuinely challenging each other as well as having highly inclusive working practices, with everyone involved.

Richard DuFour (2004, p. 6) recognised that PLCs were used to 'describe every imaginable combination of individuals with an interest in education', and that the concept 'is in danger of losing all meaning'. As such, he decided to outline the 'big ideas' that are at the foundation of PLCs, and to demonstrate how these ideas can support school colleagues in embedding the desired culture in their school networks.

Big Idea #1 is that the purpose of formal schooling is to ensure that students learn. DuFour argues that the shift in emphasis from teaching to learning has profound implications that include staff asking themselves questions such as, 'What school characteristics and practices have been most successful in helping students to achieve at high levels?' (p. 6). He suggests that the critical difference between PLCs and what he terms 'traditional schools' is the answer to the question, 'How will we respond when a student experiences difficulty in learning?' (p. 7). His answer is that a PLC should respond in a fashion that is timely, based on intervention and directive (that is, students should be required to receive additional support until they have reached the desired standard).

Big Idea #2 is that the school should foster a culture of collaboration. DuFour's interpretation of collaboration is a PLC in which teachers work together systematically to analyse and improve their classroom practice, working in teams and 'engaging in an ongoing cycle of questions that promote deep team learning' (p. 8) that, in turn, will lead to higher student achievement. He argues that educators create structures that enable this type of collaboration, for 'building the collaborative culture of a PLC is a question of will. A group of staff members who are determined to work together will find a way' (p. 9).

Big Idea #3 is a focus on results. DuFour argues that PLCs judge their effectiveness on student results, and that working together to improve student achievement becomes 'the routine work of everyone in the school' (p. 10). As a result, school aims become far more specific and relate to improving the percentage of students that reach the required grades in their examinations; teachers ask themselves how much progress they have made on the goals that are important to their PLC.

DuFour emphasises the hard work involved in initiating and sustaining the concept of a PLC; that the value of a PLC lies in 'the commitment and persistence and of the educators within it' (p. 11). Here is a crucial aspect. While there can be a collective and collaborative focus on *performance* of students, it is for the purpose of improving learning opportunities and not simply for the purpose of accountability.

It is very clear that PLCs are 'not unproblematic' in either their conceptualisation or practice, and that recognising the range of legitimate values within a complex social organisation such as a school is 'at the heart of this problematic' (Watson, 2014, p. 26). Nevertheless, if we are to embrace and encourage a collaborative culture, schools will need to wrestle with these difficulties.

Pause to reflect

Interestingly, perception of school climate and culture has had a significant impact on in-service teachers' sense of stress and has been associated with teachers' burnout (Geng, Midford & Buckworth, 2016). As such, if we want a collaborative, collegial and supportive culture, we must consider how we can optimise the probability of one forming.

Through reviewing literature around Professional Learning Communities (PLCs), consider how long you think it would take for a PLC to become 'mature'. What would help or hinder this process?

You may find the following useful as you reflect upon PLCs:

- Katz, S. (2014) *What makes a PLC effective?* Available at www.youtube.com/watch?v=PHwg5UjYE20.
- Bolam, R., McMahon, A., Stoll, L., et al. (2006). *Creating and Sustaining Effective Professional Learning Communities.* Available at http://dera.ioe.ac.uk/5622/1/RR637.pdf.

Chapter summary

Political discourse that focuses on performativity and high-stakes accountability can have unintended consequences in terms of teachers' resilience, wellbeing and perceptions of professionalism and professional identity. There needs to be a paradigm shift to *responsibility* from *accountability*. Teachers should be challenged and should feel responsible, but accountability without perceptions of control is fundamentally flawed. There needs to be a view to *sustaining* rather than *retaining* (Downey et al., 2014) teachers and their professional identity. The person and the teacher are intertwined and teachers will need *sustaining moments* (Schaefer & Clandinin, 2011). Teachers must also explicitly acknowledge political discourse and the impact of policy; they need to mediate it and position themselves within it if they are to thrive (Lea, 2013). There needs to be a culture of collegiality and collaboration that supports teachers, enabling them to thrive. Professional Learning Communities (PLCs) may be a useful concept in developing such a culture, but developing a *mature* collaborative culture is no easy task. Indeed, the challenge is to create a collaborative culture in the face of competitive and potentially isolating political drivers.

References

Adams, K., Monahan, J. & Wills, R. (2015) Losing the whole child? A national survey of primary education training provision for spiritual, moral, social and cultural development. *European Journal of Teacher Education*, 38(2), 119-216.

Apple, M.W. (2013) *Can Education Change Society?* Abingdon: Routledge.

Ball, S.J. (2003) The teacher's soul and the terrors of performativity. *Journal of Education Policy*, 18(1), 215-228.

Ball, S.J. (2004) Performativities and fabrications in the education economy:towards the performative society, in S.J. Ball (ed.), *The Routledge-Falmer Reader in Sociology of Education*. London: Routledge-Falmer.

Beck, J. (2008) Governmental professionalism: re-professionalising or de-professionalising teachers in England. *British Journal of Educational Studies*, 56(2), 119-143.

Becker, H.S. (1963) *The Outsiders: Studies in the Sociology of Deviance*. London: Free Press of Glencoe.

Beijaard, D., Meijer, P.C. & Verloop, N. (2004) Reconsidering research on teachers' professional identity. *Teaching and Teacher* Education, 20, 107-128.

Billett, S. & Pavlova, M. (2005) Learning through working life:self and individuals' agentic action. *International Journal of Lifelong Education*, 24(3), 195-211.

Blankenship, S. & Ruona, W. (2007) *Professional Learning Communities and Communities of Practice:A Comparison of Models, Literature Review. Paper presented at Academy of Human Resource Development International Research Conference in the Americas.* Available at http://files.eric.ed.gov/fulltext/ED504776.pdf.

Campbell-Barr, V. & Leeson, C. (2016) *Quality and Leadership in the Early Years:Research, Theory and Practice.* London:Sage.

Carlone, H.B., Haun-Frank, J. & Kimmel, S.C. (2010) Tempered radicals: elementary teachers' narratives of teaching science within and against prevailing meanings of schooling. *Cultural Studies of Science Education*, 6, 941-965.

Crocco, M.S. & Costigan, A.T. (2007) The narrowing curriculum and pedagogy in the age of accountability. *Urban* Education, 42, 512-535.

Downey, C.A., Schaefer, L. & Clandinin, D.J. (2014) Shifting teacher education from 'skilling up' to sustaining beginning teachers. *Learning Landscapes*, 8(1), 15-20.

DuFour, R. (2004) What is a Professional Learning Community? *Educational Leadership*, May, 6-11. Available at www.ascd.org/publications/educational-leadership/may04/vol61/num08/What-Is-a-Professional-Learning-Community%C2%A2.aspx.

Evans, L. (2008) Professionalism, professionality and the development of education professionals. *British Journal of Educational Studies*, 56(1), 20-38.

Geng, G., Midford, R. & Buckworth, J. (2016) Comparing stress levels of graduate and undergraduate pre-service teachers following their teaching practicums. *Australian Journal of Teacher Education*, 41(9).

Goodson, I (2003) *Professional Knowledge, Professional Lives: Studies in Education and Change.* Maidenhead:Open University Press.

Hall, D. & McGinity, R. (2015) Conceptualizing teacher professional identity in neoliberal times: resistance, compliance and reform. *Education Policy Analysis Archives*, 23(88), 1-17. Available at http://dx.doi.org/10.14507/epaa.v23.2092.

Hökkä, P., Vähäsantanen, K. & Mahlakaarto, S. (2017) Teacher educators' collective professional agency and identity: transforming marginality to strength. *Teaching and Teacher Education*, 63, 36-46.

Korthagen, F. (2017) Inconvenient truths about teacher learning:towards professional development 3.0. *Teachers and Teaching*, 23(4), 387-405.

Lea, S. (2013) Early years work, professionalism and the translation of policy into practice, in Z. Kingdom & J. Gourd (eds.), *Early Years Policy: The Impact of Practice.* London:Routledge.

Lee, S. and Schallert, D.L. (2016) Becoming a teacher:coordinating past, present, and future selves with perspectival understandings about teaching. *Teaching and Teacher Education*, 56, 72-83.

Lewis, K. (2014) Constructions of professional identity in a dynamic higher education sector. *Perspectives: Policy and Practice in Higher Education,* 18(2), 43–50.

Loh, J. (2013) Resistance within a performativity discourse: learning from an analytic autoethnographic perspective. *Waikato Journal of Education,* 18(2), 157–169.

Lount, R.B. (2010) The impact of positive mood on trust in interpersonal and intergroup interactions. *Journal of Personality and Social Psychology,* 98(3), 420–433.

Lukes, S. (2004) *Power: A Radical View,* 2nd ed. London: Palgrave Macmillan.

MacBlain, S., Dunn, J. & Luke, I. (2017) *Contemporary Childhood.* London: Sage.

Mansfield, C.F., Beltman, S., Broadley, T. & Weatherby-Fell, N. (2016) Building resilience in teacher education: an evidenced informed framework. *Teaching and Teacher Education,* 54, 77–87.

Maslow, A.H. (1954) *Motivation and Personality,* 3rd ed. New York: Longman.

Meyerson, D.E. (2004) The tempered radicals: how employees push their companies – little by little – to be more socially responsible. *Stanford Social Innovation Review,* Fall, 13–22.

Milner, A (2017) *The Buffer-Fly.* Paper presented at the University of St Mark & St John Research Conference, Plymouth, September.

Moss, P. (2015) There are alternatives! Contestation and hope in early childhood education. *Global Studies of Childhood,* 5(3), 226–238.

Moss, P. & Dahlberg, G. (2008) Beyond quality in early childhood education and care: languages of evaluation. *New Zealand Journal of Teachers Work,* 5(1), 3–12.

National Union of Teachers (2017) Workload driving young teachers out of the profession. Available at www.teachers.org.uk/news-events/conference-2017/workload-driving-young-teachers-out-profession.

Olivant, K.F. (2015) 'I am not a format': teachers' experiences with fostering creativity in the era of accountability. *Journal of Research in Childhood Education,* 29, 115–129.

Osgood, J. (2006) Deconstructing professionalism in early childhood education: resisting the regulatory gaze. *Contemporary Issues in Early Childhood,* 7(1), 5–14.

Osgood, J. (2010) Reconstructing professionalism in ECEC: the case for the critically reflective emotional professional. *Early Years: An International Research Journal,* 30(2), 119–133.

Ovenden-Hope, T. & Blandford, S. (2018) *Understanding Applied Learning: Developing Effective Practice to Support All Learners.* London: Routledge.

Owen, S. (2016) Professional Learning Communities: building skills, reinvigorating the passion, and nurturing teacher wellbeing and 'flourishing' within significantly innovative schooling contexts. *Educational Review*. Available at: http://dx.doi.org/10.1080/00131911.2015.1119101.

Pajak. E. (2012) Willard Waller's sociology of teaching reconsidered: 'what does teaching do to teachers?' *American Educational Research Journal*, 49(6), 1182-1213.

Roffey, S. (2012) Pupil wellbeing – teacher wellbeing: two sides of the same coin? *Educational & Child Psychology*, 29(4), 8-17.

Ryan, M. & Bourke, T. (2013) The teacher as reflexive professional: making visible the excluded discourse in teacher standards. *Discourse: Studies in the Cultural Politics of Education*, 34(3), 302-322.

Sachs, J. (2003) Teacher activism: Mobilising the profession. Available at www.researchgate.net/profile/Judyth_Sachs/publication/253589129_Teacher_Activism_Mobilising_the_Profession/links/56bba1b708ae47fa3956b1cf/Teacher-Activism-Mobilising-the-Profession.pdf.

Schaefer, L. & Clandinin, D.J. (2011) Stories of sustaining: a narrative inquiry into the experiences of two beginning teachers. *Learning Landscapes*, 4(2), 275-295.

Turner-Bisset, R. (2007) Performativity by stealth: a critique of recent initiatives on creativity. *Education 3-13*, 55(2), 193-203.

Vass, J. (2015) Selfhood and its pragmatic coherence in the context of social entropy: towards a new framework of the social self. *Contemporary Social Science*, 10(1), 26-38.

Watson, C. (2014) Effective Professional Learning Communities? The possibilities for teachers as agents of change in schools. *British Educational Research Journal*, 40(1), 18-29.

Wilkins, C. (2010) Professionalism and the post-performative teacher: new teachers reflect on autonomy and accountability in the English school system. *Professional Development in Education*, 37(3), 389-409.

2 Principled professionalism in the classroom

Suzanne Hope

Introduction

The classroom is a complex place with many competing agendas. The need to teach the curriculum and meet curriculum objectives play heavily on the teacher's mind often causing stress and anxiety (Ryan & Bourke, 2013). Performativity agendas that include attainment benchmarks, floor targets, professional development plans and related professional agendas, teacher observation and monitoring can all dominate the classroom climate. The need to maximise every moment of potential learning time can lead to classrooms that minimise the human needs of teachers and learners and pressurise both leading to anxiety, stress and potential unhappiness (Brighouse & Woods, 1999; Noddings, 2003).

Concern for the wellbeing of children has risen to a rhetoric that is voiced in reports and research but fails to be prioritised in terms of government policy. The life satisfaction of children in England was rated the lowest of 14 countries excluding South Korea in the Good Childhood Report (Children's Society, 2015) prompting many such as Roffey (2016, p. 39) to call for a relational response to young people, as she reminds us, 'for some children school may be the only place where people authentically care about them'. Ironically, she argues that schools can be a problematising place for vulnerable children who face adverse life circumstances as the institutional compliance demanded of pupils in today's performativity-obsessed schools can result in these pupils being further stigmatised, creating a 'double-whammy' (Roffey, 2016, p. 30). One of the pivotal protective factors she identifies in helping children to develop the resilience they need to cope with difficult circumstances, is the role of a caring teacher.

This chapter will explore the moral dimensions of being a 'principled professional' (Goodson, 2000) and will seek to re-legitimise the development of democracy and relational practice as a priority for the content of the curriculum, the attainment of children and the flourishing of the individuals who inhabit the classroom on a daily basis.

> **By the end of the chapter you will:**
>
> - Develop strategies that allow you to prioritise your principled professionalism.
> - Understand the nature of the challenges presented by teaching in today's classroom culture.

I'm not political - I'm a teacher

Teaching has often been construed as a vocation (Nias, 1989) embracing intrinsic motivation to nurture and care. Troman (2008) found this conception of teaching to be particularly represented by older teachers, which may be attributed to their pre-existence before the paradigm shift in educational policy that has taken place since the Conservative Government's Education Reform Act of 1988. Teachers trained after this period have had their pedagogy forged in what has been described as a culture of compliance (Alexander, 2010). Eaude (2011, p. 51) acknowledges that teaching pedagogy has been increasingly externally prescribed resulting in a, 'narrowing of children's learning experiences, in practice'.

While many scholars vehemently argue that governments have colonised teachers' professionalism, eroding teacher autonomy (Bourke, Lidstone & Ryan, 2013), it could be said that teachers have been left out of the conversation. The neoliberal *elephant in the classroom*, while widely derided by academic commentators, remains firmly in place. As teachers may feel that they are not in the business of politics, and so relentlessly yet so subtly have political mandates invaded the classroom space, that it may be quite possible that teachers have become docile and unaware of the extent to which performativity has infused the practice of teaching. Not to recognise the political infiltration of education, it could be argued, is to succumb to it.

Ironically, the professionalism of teachers, which has been so undermined, can be used as a shield to resist the political forces argues Goodson (2000) in his call for teachers to become *principled professionals*, Goodson is calling for teachers to assert a moral professionalism that is grounded not in the imposition of market forces, but in the human space that has always characterised the encounters between teacher and child. The tools of the principled professional, Goodson reminds us, include the ability to reflect; not the technical reflection of how to plan an Ofsted excellent lesson, but reflection that engages with 'the moral and social purposes and value of what teachers teach' (Goodson, 2000, p.187). His vision of teachers working in collaborative cultures to actively care for their students, and other principles he identifies, it could be argued, are echoed by many commentators today.

Principles of Goodson's Principled Professionalism (2000)

- Engage with the moral and social purposes of what teachers teach.
- Increasing the discretionary powers of teachers in decisions pertaining to teaching and students.
- Commitment to collaborative culture and practice.
- Partnering with the wider community.
- Committing to actively care for students.
- A teacher-initiated struggle to continuously learn.
- That there should be recognition of the complexity of teaching as a task and that this should be reflected in terms of status and financial reimbursement.

Teachers have a duty of care to themselves to honour their own professional integrity, and their own values in a time when the dominant educational philosophy may undermine the very ability to live according to one's values. Hufford (2011, p. 53), like many others, calls for teachers to develop a 'resistant aesthetic sensibility' in order to be, 'an independent open-minded thinker who resists being pushed into those prescriptive pedagogical boxes that negate imagination, creativity and authentic selfhood'. Such resistance may for some be too much in the parlance of the teacher *activist* but when the forces of performativity are so dominantly active within our schools and insidiously invisible as to become unquestioned, even teachers with an ethic of care may be unwitting but complicit active agents. As Scott (2012) argues, a caring teacher can be complicit in reproducing damaging institutionalising practices. A teacher who believes that she is responding in a caring way can commit symbolic violence against pupils, wholly unaware of the extent to which her values have been subsumed by her passive submission to the habits of the institution in which she teaches. An example of this may be seen in the way in which a teacher negates the humanity of a pupil by over-identifying that pupil with her perception of his ability-potential. The way of resistance to such unexplored practice can be through reflection, as Scott argues using Tripp's definition (2012) that critical incidents 'are not simply things that happen, but things that are created – they are incited' (Scott, 2012, p. 535).

Case study: shaping a defiant pupil

Paul knew he was in the lowest ability groups in his class. As a nine-year-old he had a large physical presence and was the biggest child in his Year 5 class. We were studying war and he loved the subject. He had presented the best drama improvisation in the class and had performed it based on Morpurgo's *Friend or Foe* with fluency, creativity and an authentic appreciation of time and place. He had not been happy though about being partnered with a girl, who he knew was ordained as his partner, as she often was, because she was in the same literacy group as him, 'the lowest one'.

When his peers had been reluctant to do an improvisation in front of the class, Paul had volunteered himself and his partner. For a few minutes, the class's disbelief was suspended as they both fully inhabited the characters in the novel, discovering a crashed German fighter plane while exploring Dartmoor. The fluency of their performance was not reflected in Paul's writing, the teacher later told me.

Paul's enthusiasm turned to frustration when the writing task appeared. He refused to do it and the teacher saw only defiance. When I spoke to him, he explained that he did not want to work with the girl, as 'she knew nothing about World War 2 and I know everything!'

When I suggested that I scribe with him to record what he knew, Paul's demeanour changed and a stream of consciousness flowed that demonstrated knowledge and understanding that would have marked him as an expert on the era among his peers. What started as a scribing role soon developed into the role of a co-writer as Paul, corrected me at times and was insistent in taking an active role in phrasing and expression. I was no longer writing, he was. He just did not have a pencil in his hand.

Pause to reflect

- What part did the teacher play in shaping a defiant student?
- What factors may have contributed to Paul's response?
- How could this situation have been avoided?

You may find the following article useful to consider:

- Graham, L.J. & Grieshaber, S. (2008) Reading dis/ability: Interrogating paradigms in a prism of power. *Disability & Society*, 23(6), 557–570.

When teachers give up their power – as agents of their own moral compass – they can become more vulnerable to performativity-cloaked professional development. The professionalisation of teaching favoured by successive neoliberal governments masquerades as professionalism for as Goodson

(2000) observes, control is retained by the government. Pedagogical visions have been sidelined in favour of policy missives that reduce teachers to *passive technicians*; collectors of evidence and archivers of levels.

Our education system is so coercively mired in centrally controlled diktats, that some glaring pedagogical omissions go unquestioned; for example, that children's achievement should be measured in academic terms without recourse to seeking to value or measure the holistic development and flourishing of children. What is left out of the pedagogical conversation a nation is having with itself becomes redundant and left to be recognised only by those educational dissidents who would dare to question. And yet, the wisdom of teacher practice is owned by those who daily evolve their own personal philosophy of education, embracing experience, values and filtered through the ethical gaze of one's self. In Higgins' re-assertion of the dialogical space that should surround education, we have what seems utopian given the present political and cultural context:

> Education is the ongoing conversation taking place in the space opened by the question of what best facilitates human flourishing; it consists of the explicit and implicit answers, described and enacted, by those theorists, practitioners, and theorist/ practitioners who feel called to join the conversation.
>
> (Higgins, 2010, p. 451)

Pause to reflect

Who am I who teaches?

Examining one's own values and asking 'Who am I who teaches?' (Ferguson, 2015) is one line of defence against the increasing neoliberal invasion of educational practice. Identifying assumptions that undergird how and why you teach, is an important aspect of self-validation and gives a teacher the confidence to stake professional identity when voicing the justification for pedagogical decisions. Ferguson looked to theoretical voices to develop his educational practice and assert his own educational accountability. Identifying your nexus of inspirational educational writers as Ferguson did (Freire, Foucault, McNiff and Palmer) can help to locate and clarify your own educational philosophy. While Ferguson achieved his exploration through study, it may be that reading reflectively can prove as valuable.

Finding alignment between your own values and the principles used by others to articulate their pedagogical visions can embolden the teacher and restore a sense of agency that may have been lost in practice.

Of course, there are many who are not called to join the *conversation* (e.g., the teachers, children and parents) despite the obvious tacit understanding that many of us have and that research bears out, i.e., the priority for parents and teachers, remains, *the child's happiness* (Scoffham & Barnes, 2011). Indeed, many teachers define their role in terms of hoping to play a part in helping children to be happy; it is a storyline of care that is dominant in how teachers conceptualise themselves (Shacklock, 1998; Adams, 2015).

While Adams (2015) suggests that an ethic of care in primary education policy and practice is desirable, he acknowledges that there is minimal place for it in our current system. While there will always be teachers who teach according to their own sense of ethics, there seems to be an indelible moral vacuum at the centre of today's pedagogical vision, which is affecting the ability of some teachers to recognise caring as a pedagogical responsibility. It has been argued that the technical-rationalist climate obscures teachers' ability to recognise the moral dimensions of their practice (Huebner, 1996, cited in Joseph, 2016)

While teachers may start with altruistic motivations to teach, it can be said that teacher education nullifies teachers as moral beings (Richardson & Watt, 2005, cited in Joseph, 2016) and the habitus of teaching in today's system results for some, in a praxis shock as teachers find themselves having to engage in practices that are not congruent to their value system (Loh & Hu, 2014).

Looking through a glass darkly: a teacher's reflection

I was considered to be a successful teacher. I took pride in establishing positive relationships with my pupils and I tried to inculcate a love of learning in my classroom. I considered myself to be an independent thinker who resisted some of the performativity agenda that infused the school's approach to learning, but I was becoming increasingly dissatisfied with the culture of the school in which I worked.

The tracking of pupil progress through testing and data analysis was becoming more insidious and it was becoming increasingly difficult to teach according to my own pedagogy and ethos. My love of literacy had been infectiously communicated to many of my past students but I realised that the daily conversations with the head teacher about how to 'upskill' my students was derailing my literacy vision and I was seeking the holy grail of better writing by teaching increasingly discrete skills such as how to write complex sentences.

Literacy as a way of making meaning and evolving one's own identity was being subjugated by a much more technical interpretation of literacy. I was successful in teaching children how to write well but I was aware that in this pursuit of technical skills, the opportunity for children to find out who they were and to experience creativity and fun, was being compromised, and consequently, I was losing my initial vocation as an educator.

Pause to reflect

- How could this teacher resolve the conflict in her pedagogy?
- What theorists could she have cited to justify the validity of taking a more creative approach to literacy?

Teachers' inability to align their professional selves with their personal self, mandated by the marketisation of their role, can take a toll on an individual's mental health and morale that goes unforeseen. That teaching cannot be regarded simply in terms of a teacher's behaviour and competency but should also consider beliefs, identity and mission, seems to be self-evident (Raus & Falkenberg, 2014) but the lens through which teachers are often perceived, seems to be myopic, obscuring the pivotal role played by our values. Raus and Falkenberg (2014, p. 105) reference the ecological self; a 'deepened and widened self whose identity is one that identifies with one's natural ecology into which one is embedded so that any destruction of that natural ecology is a destruction of one's self'.

A teacher who has a holistic view of the child but has to act within an instrumental arena of teaching and learning faces a paradox. As well as the burden of experiencing a state of moral crisis – for as Ball (2003, p. 224) writes, 'performance has no room for caring' – there is of course, the obvious implication using Goodson's terminology (2000), of realising that you are in danger of becoming an *unprincipled professional*.

However, while some argue that neoliberal educational reform has damaged teachers through the, 'dislocation of teachers' pedagogic and professional identities' (Smyth, Roy & Mitte, 2015, p.155), such disempowerment can, it could be argued, be countered *by teachers themselves*.

In order to be sustained and to thrive, teachers need to have an awareness of the relational aspects of education that can negate some of the neoliberal agendas and resultant pressures. Teachers need to be freed from performative guilt in order to encourage a culture of humanity and care that reflects their principles as caring professionals. Fortunately, there are those who are issuing a rallying cry to restore the relational aspects of teaching.

Pause to reflect

Read the comments from Noddings and consider their currency. Consider the importance of seeing the teacher as the catalyst for *relational practice*.

> At a time when the traditional structures of caring have deteriorated, schools must become places where teachers and students live together, talk with each other, take delight in each other's company. It is obvious that children will work harder and do things... for people they love and trust.
>
> (Noddings, 1988, cited in Roffey, 2016, p. 39)

> [T]he teacher sets an example with her whole self – her intellect, her responsiveness, her humour, her curiosity... her caring.
>
> (Noddings, 2003: 244)

The responsibility of the teacher

The responsibility upon a teacher to be the catalyst for relational practice can be seen as a weighty one as it implies a duty to act as a change agent and to engage in an ongoing transformation of pedagogy and practice. To resist the normative conception of the role of teacher-technician implies a moral obligation to landscape new educational futures and seed other pedagogical possibilities. While early career teachers may feel that they have not yet earned the right to contest policy, they need to assert the moral obligation of honouring the child with a values-infused experience of learning. Interestingly, the challenges that early career teachers face in mediating political intervention in their teaching contexts, have been documented. In a study by Adoniou (2015, p. 410), early career teachers experienced frustration in schools that 'demonstrated panic rather than intellectual investigation' as they sought to meet performance indicators.

In order to refute political interference in education and thus in one's practice, teachers need to become articulate and replace the voices of government ministers with respected educational scholars. This involves a personal as well as a professional challenge; Noddings (2013) argues that to develop children as deliberative thinkers, teachers need to become deliberative thinkers themselves and interrogate school and government policy. The critique that Noddings offers successfully interrogates some of the painful prongs of performativity; for example, she suggests that it is more apt for a teacher to consider herself *responsible* rather than *accountable*, for 'accountability points upward in the hierarchy and tends to direct teachers' attention to their own vulnerability for rewards and penalties' (Noddings, 2013, p.8) and instead reminds us that we have only ethical responsibility for the care of our students.

If teachers are to honour this responsibility then there is a moral obligation to voice objection to the significant harm that has been done to children as a result of school reform based on standards and testing. Noddings is not alone in acknowledging that our present educational system brutalises generations of children in terms of neglecting to consider that self-esteem, experience of school and childhood, could all be casualties in the race for standards. While some authors such as Karin Murris, accuse the system of perpetrating an 'ontoepistemic injustice' (Murris, 2016, p.xi) against children by refusing them agency in their own learning, the reality is that schooled practice remains oblivious to such calls.

The principled professionalism of an individual teacher may be the most realistic counterweight to counterbalance some of the negative connotations of political interference in the teacher's world. Murris (2013) calls for us to *really listen to* the child, and in order to do this we must reconsider the relationship between the child and the adult. Murris suggests that, 'adults often put metaphorical sticks in their ears in their educational encounters with children' (2013, p. 245). Her call to reject past educational visions that subjugated the child to a position of passivity and disempowerment is one that fits well with the futuristic projections of what a child in the 21st century needs to become. Of course, such a conceptual leap has to be first made by the teacher and her teaching configured to serve this newly conceptualised being. If we are to listen to the children in *our* relational space, then this has implications for our teaching context that cannot be satisfied by centrally positioned policymakers.

Pause to reflect

What does your view of professionalism embrace?
Rather than deriving your understanding of the meaning of professionalism solely from the interpretation of professional standards, consider scholarly discussion such as Wilson et al. (2013, cited in Waring & Evans, 2015), who suggest that to more deeply and critically probe, reflect upon the following:

- Is your view of professionalism externally or internally determined or an integration of both?
- How much awareness do you have of the impact of your actions on colleagues and pupils?

- Does it focus more on rights or responsibilities?
- Is your professionalism an external persona for the workplace or is it a part of your self-identity?
- Does your teaching embrace a technical-rationalist approach to what works or is it more informed by pedagogical theory and rational and intuitive decision-making?

You may find the following useful in your reflections:

- Waring, M. & Evans, E. (2015) *Understanding Pedagogy: Developing a Critical Approach to Teaching and Learning*. Oxon: Routledge.

Stay true to your teaching context and your pupils

School reform predicated too much on policy can lead to a school that attributes no value to its context and seeks to derive its identity from government mandate, which can lead to it finding itself bereft of identity. Hlebowitsh (2012) warns of the fallacy of teaching based on 'best practices' that are often derived from a place removed from the ecologically sound and personally known places of our own classroom. 'Professional judgement... should never take such a large step away from its constituency' (Hlebowitsh, 2012, p. 11).

Noddings (2003, p. 244) suggests that teachers be lead more by respecting the context in which they teach: 'What form or level of learning is called for *this* topic, for *this* student, in *this* situation?'

This approach constitutes a pedagogical challenge of *responding to individual children, to the children with whom you have established a relationship*. It is in this moral realm that a teacher is responsible; for establishing a connection with a child that ignites a love of learning and that enables that child to embark upon a lifelong journey, of which school is just a start. The professional challenge is that a teacher has no mandated curriculum but needs to respond to qualitative factors such as what the children want to learn about or what their environment provides as stimulus for their curiosity. This may not be measurable, transferable or suitable for generation to other contexts and that, perhaps, is its failing, for it is its intrinsic lack of efficiency and resistance to standardisation that puts such an approach beyond the desires of policymakers.

Teaching democratically

This relational space is one in which children are positioned democratically as participants in their own learning. How we inscribe power in our relations with children is a moral question and as Noddings (2013) asserts, we must model caring, and our own behaviour as we interact with pupils must reflect our moral selves. This teacherly self has to negotiate and resist the overly performative professionalised self in order to honour the special place of relational encounter that teachers know. Noddings reminds us of how human such contact has to be; 'Eye contact, a smile, a raised finger of caution, a gentle reminder, a disappointed frown... are all responses that recognize the student as a special, particular human being' (2013, p.120).

Reconfiguring our approach can also reinvigorate other areas of teacher activity; if a teacher empowers the children to take some leadership in shaping the curriculum to suit their interests and their experiences, they may be liberated from the behavioural need to control or *manage* the children. The fluctuations in power that a teacher enables in their classroom will redefine more normative conceptions of teaching, including the relationship that a teacher has with their pupils. When children are allowed to enjoy the autonomy to which they are entitled, a different atmosphere within a class can ensue. When they are asked to evolve the culture within the class, when they enjoy student-centred curriculum integration, and when they enjoy the concept of democracy in practice, normative notions of relationship change. This adaption is a cultural one involving action. Brough (2012, p. 364), who observed teachers attempting to implement democratic principles, reported that, 'the teachers shifted from talking about democracy to thinking democratically and acting democratically'.

Teaching democratically may be an antidote for both teachers and children in today's classrooms; this approach may be a way of a creating a subtle but nonetheless powerful *terrain of resistance*; a way of being in our classrooms while staying true to ourselves and to the children. Interestingly, there are teachers who are resisting performativity practices, as Ball and Olmedo (2013, p.85) report, although they are not engaged in an epochal confrontation, but in a 'struggle against mundane, quotidian neoliberalisations', thinking about education and the opportunity to do things *differently*.

It could be argued that a good starting point is to reinstate the child at the centre of the schooled experience. Instead of being shunted into the peripheral borderlands of the neoliberal approach to schooling, where assessment, accountability and curriculum dominate the landscape, the child can be recalled. If learning outcomes were centred upon generating positive emotions in the children, then we are more likely to *see* children flourishing and teachers thriving. Planning for happiness might then seem logical and not absurd. Some key principles to inspire a teacher are offered at the end of the chapter.

Frustration with the current system may be stimulating research that explores ways of improving children's wellbeing at school. An investigation into the impact of creative partnerships in schools by Galton and Page (2015) found that the relational realities of the schools had the potential to be transformed; these included the aspirations of the children; of changing the teachers' perceptions of the children and the pupils' perceptions of the teachers. Further claims are made of the positive impact upon the children's self-confidence, self-esteem and wellbeing. Perhaps most interesting is that the projects are evaluated in terms that transcend the *inspection* practice; citing possible gains in pupil autonomy, self-regulation and possibility thinking. Most promising is the authors' suggestion that creative partnerships within schools can result in the construct of school connectedness proposed by McNeely, Nonnemaber and Blum (2002, cited in Galton & Page, 2015), which positions pupils as individuals and gives them autonomy and a sense of belonging to a learning community. Such approaches go far beyond meeting the cognitive needs of our children and aim instead, for cognitive needs to be met in a holistic way that has psychological wellbeing as its ultimate outcome.

Ultimately, a teacher's responsibility is to nurture her students, by recognising their potentiality and by not conflating a child's potentiality with ability groups or over-identifying a child with limiting labels. If a teacher overly categorises a child's ability, she can be negating their identity and nulling their value as human and precious (see the Case study: Shaping a defiant pupil). There has to be a reciprocity of respect and trust between pupil and teacher, and often what can appear to be behaviour challenges on the part of children are simply a child's recognition of the teacher's willingness to dehumanise them made manifest. Children, like adults, are aware when dignity and kindness are not afforded to them.

Chapter summary

This chapter has wrestled with some of the issues that teachers can explore in order to make their classrooms enjoyable places to be. Paying attention to the relational aspects of education improves relationships and can moderate behaviour; however, this takes time and the teacher has to take time to learn to really listen to children and develop classroom democracy based on mutual respect and trust (Noddings, 2003). Without this the performative efforts of teachers are likely to fail or at best be less successful (Watson, Emery & Bayliss, 2012). For some teachers, all of this comes naturally but for others the conditioning through meeting teacher standards when in training and through regular focused observation by management throughout the newly qualified and early career years negates the importance of the intuitive principles of the professional and develops a *regime of truth* over time allocation, marking, assessment and feedback (Bourke et al., 2013).

The invitation to be politically aware is no longer a polite one. As Adoniou (2015, p.412) concludes, 'it is teachers who see the consequences of educational policy initiatives played out in classrooms and if they are not equipped to speak and act on what they see – who will?'

References

Adams, P. (2015) In defence of care: Gilligan's relevance for primary education. *Pedagogy, Culture & Society*, 23(2), 281–300.

Adoniou, M. (2015) 'It's very much taken as an insult if I say anything': do new educators have a right to speak their mind? *Cambridge Journal of Education*, 45(4), 401–414.

Alexander, R. (ed.) (2010) *Children, their World, their Education: Final Report and Recommendations of the Cambridge Primary Review*. London: Routledge.

Ball, S.J. (2003) The teacher's soul and the terrors of performativity. *Journal of Education Policy*, 18, 215–228.

Ball, S.J. & Olmedo, A. (2013) Care of the self, resistance and subjectivity under neoliberal governmentalities. *Critical Studies in Education*, 54(1), 85–96.

Bourke, T., Lidstone K. & Ryan, M. (2013) Schooling teachers: professionalism or disciplinary power? Educational Philosophy and Theory, 47(1), 84–100.

Brighouse, T. & Woods, D. (1999) *How to Improve Your School*. London: Routledge.

Brough, C.J. (2012) Implementing the democratic principles and practices of student-centred curriculum integration in primary schools. *Curriculum Journal*, 23(3), 345–369.

Children's Society (2015) *The Good Childhood Report 2015*. Available at http://goodchildhood2015.childrenssociety.org.uk.

Eaude, T. (2011) Compliance or innovation? Enhanced professionalism as the route to improving learning and teaching. *Education Review*, 24(1), 49–57.

Ferguson, P.B. (2015) Who am I who teaches? *Educational Journal of Living Theories*, 8(1), 49–66.

Galton, M. & Page, C. (2015) The impact of various creative initiatives on well-being: a study of children in English primary schools. *Cambridge Journal of Education*, 45(3), 349–369.

Goodson, I. (2000) The principled professional. *Prospects*, 30(2), 182–188

Higgins, C. (2010) Teaching as experience: toward a hermeneutics of teaching and teacher education. *Journal of Philosophy of Education*, 44(2/3), 435–478.

Hlebowitsh, P. (2012) When best practices aren't: a Schwabian perspective on teaching. *Journal of Curriculum Studies*, 44(1), 1–12.

Hufford, D. (2011) The educational foundations classroom and resistant aesthetic sensibility. *Journal of Philosophy & History of Education*, 61, 53–70.

Joseph, P.B. (2016) Ethical reflections on becoming teachers. *Journal of Moral Education*, 45(1), 31–45.

Loh, J. & Hu, G. (2014) Subdued by the system: neoliberalism and the beginning teacher. *In Teaching and Teacher Education*, 41, 13–21.

Murris, K. (2013) The epistemic challenge of hearing child's voice. *Studies in Philosophy & Education*, 32(3), 245–259.

Murris, K. (2016) *The Posthuman Child: Educational Transformation Through Philosophy with Anthony Browne's Little Beauty*. Abingdon: Routledge.

Nias, J. (1989) *Primary Teachers Talking*. London: Routledge.

Noddings, N. (1988) Schools face crisis in caring. *Education Week*, 8(14), 32.

Noddings, N. (2003) Is teaching a practice? *Journal of Philosophy of Education*, 37(2), 241-251.

Noddings, N. (2013) *Education and Democracy in the 21st Century*. New York: Teachers College Press.

Raus, R. & Falkenberg, T. (2014) The journey towards a teacher's ecological self: a case study of a student teacher. *Journal of Teacher Education for Sustainability*, 16(2), 103-114.

Roffey, S (2016) Building a case for whole-child, whole-school wellbeing in challenging contexts. *Educational & Child Psychology*, 33(2), 30-42.

Ryan, M. & Bourke, T. (2013) The teacher as reflexive professional: making visible the excluded discourse in teacher standards. *Discourse: Studies in The Cultural Politics of Education*, 34(3), 411-423.

Scoffham, S. & Barnes, J. (2011) Happiness matters: towards a pedagogy of happiness and well-being. *Curriculum Journal*, 22(4), 535-548.

Scott, B.C. (2012) Caring teachers and symbolic violence: engaging the productive struggle in practice and research. *Educational Studies*, 48, 530-549.

Shacklock, G. (1998) Professionalism and intensification in teaching: a case study of care in teachers' work. *Asia-Pacific Journal of Teacher Education*, 26(3), 177-189.

Smyth, J., Roy, F. & Mitte, J.C. (2015) Policy research and 'damaged teachers': towards an epistemologically respectful paradigm. *Waikato Journal of Education*, 2382-0373, 153-168.

Troman, G. (2008) Primary teacher identity, commitment and career in performative school cultures. *British Educational Research Journal*, 34(5), 619-633.

Tripp, D. (2012) *Critical Incidents in Teaching*. Oxon: Routledge.

Waring, M. & Evans, E. (2015) *Understanding Pedagogy: Developing a Critical Approach to Teaching and Learning*. Oxon: Routledge.

Watson, D., Emery, C. & Bayliss, P. (2012) *Children's Social and Emotional Wellbeing in Schools: A Critical Perspective*. Bristol: Policy Press.

3 Developing a professional identity as a teacher

Sally Eales and Anne Bradley

Introduction

This chapter will explore the concept of professional identity and how this relates to a trainee or beginning teacher's own personal values, reasons for coming into teaching and own experiences both as a pupil in school and during training. The challenges of being both a learner and a teacher will also be considered and how these work together to form and re-form professional identities over time (Livingston & Di Nardo, 2016). Some of the tensions often experienced will be considered in relation to the interplay between personal commitment and lifestyle and professional demands and suggestions will be made to enable teachers to develop strategies to manage these tensions.

By the end of the chapter you will:

- Develop an understanding of your own professional identity and how this is constructed over time.
- Understand the nature of the challenges of being a learner and a teacher.
- Consider the tensions caused by the interplay of commitment and demands and develop strategies to enable you to manage these tensions.

Teaching is highly complex involving a diverse range of skills and knowledge, underpinned by beliefs and values. Teaching also has a strong personal and emotional dimension and the interplay of these factors along with a key focus on relationships makes teaching a challenging yet satisfying profession. These components, combined with individual personal histories, result in each teacher being unique and individual. This is one of the things that makes teaching so engaging for both learners and teachers alike. Coupled with the variety of curriculum, policy and different contexts in which a teacher will work, teaching is a rich and complex job, but one that presents its own challenges. These are integral in the shaping of a teacher's professional identity.

These factors also reflect some of the reasons why new teachers seek to join the profession. Most trainee teachers express a desire to 'make a difference' or inspire children and are very often influenced by their own experience of schooling, usually positive but sometimes negative, and many will reflect on a particular teacher who inspired them as a learner. This sometimes helps develop a keen interest in a particular subject which has fuelled a particular passion and this could lead them into secondary teaching where they can particularly focus on that interest. Others remember the caring, nurturing side of a particular teacher, someone who really believed in them or helped them to overcome specific difficulties or barriers. These are often some of the reasons why teaching has a particular draw for them and many indicate that it is always something they have wanted to do and find it more difficult to pinpoint specific reasons.

Many teachers view teaching as a vocation, a lifelong career, although Troman (2008) found that this was more typical among older teachers and that younger entrants into the profession often did not consider it in this light, but viewed it as a more short-term career choice. Key factors as to why teachers join the profession underpin the development of a professional identity as these are often linked to core values and beliefs.

Case study: reflection on why an NQT wanted to become a teacher

Whenever I am asked the question 'why did you want to teach when you first applied?', it always draws my mind back to the inspiring teachers I encountered in my own schooling and the impact they have had on me. If it wasn't for those teachers, I would not be where I am today – a budding, young NQT ready to step out into the scary world of the teaching profession. Just as these teachers inspired me to persevere in my learning and achieve my goals, I wanted to be able to inspire our future generation and allow them to realise their potential – both academically and socially. I know from my own experiences of school that it is a pivotal time in a child's life, thus should be one of the most fun, inspiring, thought-provoking times. As I consider myself an out-going and fun individual, with a passion for sharing my knowledge and excitement and with a love of working with children, teaching was the most interesting and rewarding career path to pursue.

Pause to reflect

Consider your own reasons for wanting to become a teacher. Are your beliefs about how children learn influenced by your own experiences as a learner? How do you view yourself as a teacher both within the school and in wider society? Do you view teaching as a vocation or in another way? What are your feelings about being a teacher?

A trainee or beginning teacher's views are strongly influenced by a number of factors including their own experiences of learning, schools and other educational experiences (Feinman-Nemser, 2001, cited in Livingstone and Di Nardo, 2016). These help shape their views of what they perceive a *good teacher* to be and help them to determine what they might aspire to be like themselves. There is a significant amount written on what constitutes a good, effective or expert teacher (Alexander, 2010; Eaude, 2012; Hattie, 2012; Coe, Aloisi, Higgins & Major, 2014) and part of the ongoing development for teachers is matching their own experiences with what they read and know about good or expert teachers. How these align is part of the process of developing a professional identity.

A new teacher's core values may also be related to how they view the building and sustaining of personal relationships as well as how they regard the potential of all children to develop and succeed regardless of their background or ability. This will be strongly aligned to the concept of whether intelligence is fixed or can be developed (Dweck, 2008) and this will be considered in more detail later in the chapter. All these views and beliefs in turn are likely to be determined by family, cultural or religious influences and are closely intertwined with personality traits and a sense of self.

Values are clearly considered to be of significant importance in teaching (Pollard, 2014) and this notion is reflected in the professional values and behaviours for teachers that are outlined in the professional codes of conduct by many countries. These include the General Teaching Councils of Scotland and Northern Ireland, the Education Workforce Council in Wales and the Teaching Council of Ireland and within the Preamble to the Teachers' Standards (DfE, 2012) in England.

There are common themes evident related to honesty, integrity, respect, trust and care, along with expectations for collaborative working and responsibility for professional conduct and development. These provide a framework within which practice should be conducted and while it is noted that there will be differences in interpretation (Livingstone and Di Nardo, 2016), they provide key areas for consideration and discussion for the new teacher. They also call us to question what these mean in practice, in day-to-day

Table 3.1 Professional Standards for Teachers

England:
www.gov.uk/government/uploads/system/uploads/attachment_data/file/283566/
Teachers_standard_information.pdf

Scotland:
www.gtcs.org.uk/professional-standards/professional-standards.aspx

Wales:
http://learning.gov.wales/docs/learningwales/publications/140630-revised-
   professional-standards-en.pdf

Northern Ireland:
www.gtcni.org.uk/index.cfm/area/information/page/profstandard

---

teaching situations, and to be willing to test out if our own values align with what is expected of qualified teachers working in maintained schools (Pollard, 2014).

Pause to reflect

Reflect on the values and beliefs you have about teaching, how pupils learn, building relationships, equality and inclusion. How do you think these affect the way you interact with colleagues and pupils? What experiences have you had in school where you have had to put some of this into practice? Reflect on these experiences and how you may have changed your views as a result.

The integration of personal and professional lives within the teacher's identity is a strong theme recognised by many commentators (Nias, 1989; Day, Kington, Stobart & Sammons, 2006a; Pillen, Beijaard & den Brok, 2013; Gu, 2014) and also recognised within the codes of conduct mentioned previously. It is clear within the Teachers' Standards (2012) that teachers must 'uphold public trust in the profession and maintain high standards of ethics and behaviour, within and outside school' and in the Teaching Council of Ireland's Code of Professional Conduct (2016, p.7) that a teacher must 'avoid conflict between their professional work and private interests which could reasonably be deemed to impact negatively on pupils/students'. This interplay of personal and professional conduct and how individual and collective values and beliefs impact upon behaviours and outcomes reiterates that there is a clear recognition that by becoming a teacher you are signing up to certain values and expectations that need to be upheld throughout your entire career (Carroll & Alexander, 2016).

What is professional identity?

A teacher's professional identity is the way a teacher perceives him/her-self as a professional in 'the classroom, the school, the community and the society' (Gu, 2014, p. 5). Pollard (2014) recognises that beginning teachers often separate out their personal and professional selves, and stresses the importance of the formation and development of a professional iden-tity. Research into this area has developed considerably over the past two decades and has approached the question of identity from many different perspectives, but there is clear agreement that 'the events and experiences in the personal lives of teachers are intimately linked to the performance of their professional roles' (Day et al., 2006a, p. 603). Nias (1989) found that early career teachers still separated out the personal (or 'substantial') and the professional (or 'social') selves, while more experienced teachers had incorporated them and essentially viewed 'being a teacher' as 'being your-self'. However, this was linked much more strongly to the notion of 'inte-grating personal and professional connections between the teacher and the pupil' (Day et al., 2006a, p. 604) rather than in carrying out the prac-tical tasks related to teaching. If personal and professional identities align, then teaching is much more likely to be a fulfilling and worthwhile job and longer-term career prospects are enhanced (Pollard, 2014). This underlines the very strong investment of personal emotion in teaching and in building and sustaining relationships with pupils and colleagues (Gu, 2014). As Hargreaves reminds us:

> Good teaching is charged with positive emotion. It is not just a matter of knowing one's subject, being efficient, having the correct competencies, or learning all the right techniques. Good teachers are not just well-oiled machines. They are emotional, passionate beings who connect with their students and fill their work and their classes with pleasure, creativity, challenges and joy.
>
> (Hargreaves, 1998, p. 835, cited in
> Cushman & Cowan, 2010, p. 82)

Olsen (2010, cited in Pillen et al., 2013) asserted the importance of developing a professional identity in becoming a successful teacher, and the connections between teacher effectiveness and identity are considered to be signifi-cant (Day et al., 2006b). This is linked to ensuring the balance between the personal and professional aspects of identity are aligned and regulated as changing personal and professional circumstances, and how we react to them will have an impact upon this. If a teacher is experiencing changes in their home life, this can impact upon their role in school and their profes-sional identity will be affected by this. This could be short-term or may have a longer-lasting impact.

While personal and professional experiences will influence the notion of professional identity, context is also a very important factor. Where we work and who we work with will have a significant impact on how we develop as teachers. The ethos and values of a school, the pupils and the relationships formed with them, the senior management and colleagues we work closely with, will all make an important impression and for the beginning teacher this will be particularly formative. Our own opinions and views, perhaps formed from those elements outlined above, are likely to be questioned and challenged as our own expectations change and we learn more, both theoretically and practically.

Professional identities are therefore influenced by personal histories and experiences, beliefs and values, and the notion of professionalism and the situations in which we find ourselves. All of these will have an impact upon how we view ourselves as professionals and how we reconcile the differences we may experience in the different spheres of our lives. As this is constantly changing, then it is generally agreed that professional identity is not a stable entity and is clearly affected by political, social and institutional changes (Day et al., 2006a; Pillen et al., 2013). Some would argue that this has become more and more challenging in recent years as the notion of teachers' professionalism has been redefined (Ball, 2003; Tröhler, 2017) and teachers have been 'de-professionalized' and 're-professionalized' (Seddon, 1997, cited in Ball, 2003, p. 218) and that, in fact, primary teachers now need to develop much more complex identities in response to the rapidly changing world in which we live (Troman, 2008). With higher levels of institutional and collective responsibility to meet ever-changing political and social demands, this can present different kinds of issues for teachers at all stages of their careers.

Challenges of learner and teacher

As teachers develop their personal identities within the profession, it is appropriate to accept the challenges of being both a teacher and a learner. Throughout training and through experiences in schools, teachers' own ideologies change and develop. Values are shaped by multiple experiences and a teacher's personal beliefs influence how they teach (Muijs & Reynolds, 2011).

Every teacher will certify to the fact that, in this profession, one never stops learning. In fact this is one of the delights of the job: the opportunities to constantly develop knowledge and understanding not only of the world but of the children and people with whom one works. Teachers are lead learners and this in turn brings its own tensions as there are always the expectations of others to consider. There are also the tensions of being accountable to external forces driven by testing results and inspection expectations (Ball, 2003; Troman, 2008).

Pause to reflect

Reflect on your experiences as a learner. Think of yourself as a learner in school and then as a learner as you train to teach or develop professionally. What are your challenges? What are you excited by? What daunts you?

As a learner and a lead learner it is relevant to remember that learning processes do not fundamentally change from childhood to adulthood and that pedagogy enables a lead learner to use the most effective methods when planning to teach (TLRP, 2006, cited in Eaude, 2012). Shulman (2004) discusses the notion of pedagogical content knowledge (PCK) as the way in which a teacher presents material to children so that learning takes place. This is not just about having strong subject knowledge but knowing how to help children learn this knowledge. What teachers do well is plan their objectives and then respond to a child's learning (Eaude, 2012). However, the importance is not in meeting short-term needs but in developing learning that lays foundations for the future (Cooper & McIntyre, 1996). This point is developed by Pollard (2014, p.170) who suggests that a reflective professional will have, 'a short-term focus on pupil performance in relation to curriculum tasks and also a longer-term responsibility to foster each child's personal confidence as a learner'. It is the responsibility of the teacher to help children develop positive attitudes to learning.

On entering the classroom, teachers have to know and understand a wide range of matters: the age, abilities and natures of the children; the subject knowledge of what they are going to teach; the previous experiences of the children and the very best teaching approach to meet their learners' needs. An examination of part one of the Teachers' Standards presents the requirements of a qualified teacher.

The Standards clearly present the teacher's responsibility to promote the value of scholarship, a love of learning and intellectual curiosity (Blatchford, 2015). Within the Standards a teacher must also demonstrate understanding of the learning needs of all children and how to effectively meet these needs through planning, teaching, assessment and classroom management. However, teaching is so much more than meeting Standards. Cooper and McIntyre (1996) discuss the notion of teachers developing 'professional craft knowledge'. By this they refer to the experience gained through classroom practice where teachers learn to meet varying needs and to solve problems by their individual approaches. This craft is developed and honed through experience and is the result of reflection and practical problem-solving. Teachers develop their expertise to see the standards 'in terms of well-being and character, not just academic subjects' (Eaude, 2012, p. 55). Teachers are meeting the required standards and their professional responsibilities but are also using skills refined by their own understanding and experience, underpinned by their personal values.

We can see these standards as opportunities to maintain and refine our core values. Learning never stops and it is important that children see this. Teaching is not about delivery, and never has been, and by examining the ideas in studies undertaken by researchers such as Gerver (2012) and Hattie (2012) we can explore possibilities to enable children to become lifelong learners. Goodson (2000, p. 187) believes that, 'a new professionalism and body of knowledge can be driven by a belief in social practice and moral purpose'. By understanding the research undertaken to develop children as learners we can embrace some ideas to support our own principles.

If children are aware that their teachers are learning too they are more likely to engage in the process. Hattie (2012) celebrates the 'passionate teacher' who seeks to see learning through the eyes of the child. He talks about visible learning in which the child has opportunities to develop their own learning and in which the teacher shares their intentions with the children. This is as a result of positive interaction between teacher and children. If the teacher is seen to be learning too then the child will enjoy the pursuit of further challenge. Dweck (2008, p. 201) comments that after discussions with students, she found that they value teachers who learn, stating that, 'a good teacher is one who continues to learn with the students'. Hattie, in discussing the notion of an 'expert teacher' as opposed to an 'experienced teacher', suggests that:

> Experts possess knowledge that is more integrated, in that they combine the introduction of new subject knowledge with students' prior knowledge; they can relate current lesson content to other subjects in the curriculum; and they make lessons uniquely their own by changing, combining and adding to lessons according to their students' own needs and their own teaching goals.
>
> (Hattie, 2012, p. 25)

In doing this, he suggests that teachers can be more reactive to classroom events and influence surface- and more importantly, develop deep-learning outcomes. Creative and effective teaching that embraces a broad curriculum will enable children to develop deep learning strategies (Polesel, 2014).

Gerver (2012, p. 21) expresses concerns that our current educational system de-contextualises learning and he advocates that we must, 'look to think more creatively about the way we package the learning to make it exciting, relevant and dynamic'. These are inspiring aims and many young teachers enter the profession holding such values. He talks of the positive aspects of failure and that we are in danger, as a society, of seeing failure as something to be avoided rather than a signpost to risk and creativity. In his research he encouraged children to take ownership of their classroom environments and work in partnership with their teacher. He fears that our current system engenders a lack of empowerment in society. This echoes ideas on building learning power suggested by Claxton, Chambers, Powell and Lucas (2012), in which they advocate developing children's 'resilience, resourcefulness, reflectiveness and reciprocity'. By developing these aspects of learning, children do not fear failure but learn from it, they begin to understand learning and develop themselves as learners, becoming confident in a changing world. Dweck (2008, p. 15) writes about having a 'changeable ability that can be developed through learning', she calls this 'growth mind-set' and believes we can encourage children to seek challenge and learn from mistakes rather than fear failure and compare themselves to others. Teachers can promote growth mind-set by setting high standards and enabling all children to strive to achieve. Gerver (2012) also reminds us that we are educating citizens of the future, not only developing their resilience but embracing their skills. For example, children are already very adept with ICT and will be using these skills in the global marketplace. Teachers can use technology to be exciting, relevant and dynamic, and children can take a lead in this learning.

Cooper and McIntyre (1996, p. 154) believe that a distinctive feature of teachers' professional craft is, 'a concern with pupil engagement' and that high value is placed on 'strategies that stimulated pupils to be personally engaged with the lesson content'. If schools only focus upon academic instruction and, in some cases, predominantly on mathematics and literacy they will have a negative impact on children's engagement (Cushman & Cowan, 2010; Eaude, 2012, Polesel, 2014). Teachers are creative (Nias, 1989) and this aspect of the role is one of the most satisfying. By embracing flexibility, a teacher can adapt and modify a lesson to seize an opportunity to extend a discussion or develop a learning point (Eaude, 2012).

Tensions: interplay between commitment and demands

The interplay between personal values and ideologies and the particular educational context in which a teacher works also shapes and develops the professional identity and this has often been considered in the light of performative school cultures and external reform events (Troman, 2008). These are the expectations of others. We live in a time of regularly changing curriculums, inspection regulations, government policies and political influences creating expectations, set by others, for teachers to follow. Senior leaders are under pressures to ensure that these expectations are being met. This then contributes to the discussion on how stable or unstable these identities are and how these identities can be particularly shaped in initial teacher training and the early years of teaching. The work of Pillen et al. (2013) explores the tensions, accompanying feelings and coping strategies associated with beginning teachers, with a strong recognition of the emotional investment in teaching. They discuss the importance of finding a balance, understanding that teachers want to invest time in teaching but feel increasingly pressurised to spend time on other tasks such as data collection and administrative duties. They advocate that working with others, sharing information and seeking advice is an important strategy to help to cope with these pressures. Eaude (2012, p.59) suggests this as 'seeking the wisdom of others', for as Pillen et al. (2013) acknowledge, a teacher feels more confident when they realise their experiences are shared by others. Goodson (2000) in his outline of seven proposals advocates that teachers commit to working collaboratively with colleagues, sharing expertise and solving ongoing problems of professional practice. This discourse is healthy and relevant as there is joint understanding of a personal working environment that cannot possibly be acknowledged by external mandates and by the fact that every school has its own distinctive needs. He continues by recommending extending this collaboration to working with the wider community: the children themselves, other partners and parents, because everyone 'has a significant stake in the students' learning' (p.187). He stresses the importance of teachers taking control of their own 'continuous learning', which is linked to their personal interests and expertise rather than being driven by the 'endless change' from external forces (p.187). This is echoed in the ideas of Gerver (2012), Hattie (2012) and Dweck (2008).

The current focus on the professional conduct of teachers as outlined in Part 2 of the Teachers Standards (2013) supports the interplay of personal and professional commitment and how individual and collective values and beliefs impact upon behaviour and outcomes (Carroll & Alexander, 2016).

A teacher has a duty to maintain high standards of professional and personal conduct and the relationships that teachers develop in school uphold these standards. Trainee and newly qualified teachers are concerned with managing classroom behaviour and can fear loss of classroom control. This is particularly pertinent in a climate where accountability is high. For a teacher to earn the respect of the children they work with, they need to develop a relationship based on mutual understanding and empathy. Children need to understand and recognise the 'nature' of their own teacher. Students are more likely to behave well for a teacher with whom they share positive values (Goodman, 2009). He understands that teachers earn a child's respect and that a child responds to a teacher more readily through respect than through fear. One of the most valuable things a teacher can give a child is a sense of self-worth (Cushman & Cowan, 2010). By developing a climate of mutual respect and understanding, self-confidence is given an opportunity to grow. Their research also indicated that if a child is successful in one area, the self-confidence gained will lead to success in other skills. Eaude (2012) reflects that if a child is fearful in school, this undermines their skills of intuition and improvisation. Confidence comes from self-belief and a teacher is well placed to engender this.

> **Case study: thoughts of an NQT on 'What I wish I'd known on entering the profession'**
>
> One thing I know now that I wished I had known then is that there is no such thing as *perfect* in teaching. This was something told to me by my tutor in my final teaching placement when I was making myself stressed over the neatness of my placement folders and planning, and is something I still have to remind myself of now that I am teaching full-time. It really does not matter if your timetables aren't colour-coded to your folders or your planning is not perfectly aligned or that everything on your to-do list is not ticked off by the end of the day/week. All that matters is that you are healthy and happy, and that the children in your class are learning and are happy and healthy themselves. If you leave no time for yourself, this will soon start to trickle into your teaching, which can result in negative experiences for you and the children. This means prioritising is vital, especially when it comes to your own health and wellbeing. After all, a happy teacher means happy children!

It is in the nature of most teachers to *nurture* and primary teachers learn to live with the tensions of their role (Nias, 1989, p.196). At first this is not a cheerful thought but when you consider that Nias's research took place many years ago it is worth reflecting that tensions are part of the role and it is how a teacher learns to manage them that is key to their fulfilment and success. Ball (2003) discusses the paradox of a role in which a teacher is continually problem-solving and thinking creatively but is monitored and required to work within a narrowing curriculum. He feels that there is the danger of a teacher feeling insecure, not really being aware of what aspects of their job are valued. He calls this 'values schizophrenia' (p.221). Teachers who can create an environment where deep learning takes place are teachers who are meeting the correct standards and maintaining their own values. Such an environment can be co-created with the children (Cushman & Cowan, 2010). Hattie (2012, p.24) talks of inspired teachers who are 'proficient at creating an optimal classroom climate'. These teachers believe that their children can meet the success criteria and they strive to provide excellent feedback to monitor and extend learning.

Developing a professional identity over time

As we can see, the role of the teacher is complex and multifaceted, and for trainee and beginning teachers this can seem rather overwhelming at times as they grapple with what can appear to be conflicting expectations and demands from senior management, pupils, parents and the wider community.

In terms of developing a professional identity, the challenges can begin in initial teacher education (Pollard, 2014) where trainees could find themselves reconciling the approaches or underpinning philosophy of the provider or the school in which they are on placement with their own. Early on they are called to question and consider their own viewpoints in the light of different experiences, often confidently demonstrated by experienced professionals. As Pillen et al. (2013, p. 243) point out, this can be emotionally demanding as the beginning teacher begins to recognise that different approaches do not need to be mutually exclusive and that while we may not always find a solution, we need to 'find a way to cope with it'. This is going to be a common experience in a teacher's career, particularly if they move schools and take on new roles, but one that they must learn to deal with in order to grow and mature. Day et al. (2006a, p. 608) refer to these experiences as 'the shifting sands of personal experience and school cultures on which identities are constructed, deconstructed and reconstructed in the early years of teaching'.

Several researchers have considered the stages that teachers go through within their careers and it is reassuring as a beginning teacher to appreciate that there is often a common pattern. Pollard (2014) cites several models that move from early idealisation and personal survival through to different stages of consolidation, professional confidence and greater experimentation. What is clear in all of these is the understanding that there will be professional tensions throughout our careers and that those will be partly determined by the stage of career as well as our personal and professional situations. This is shared by other professions and is particularly aligned with nursing and social work where tensions in the early stages are often very similar. Pillen et al. (2013, p. 254) drew together the key tensions beginning teachers experienced and found that the most prominent focused on the three key areas:

- the conflict between caring for pupils/ students and 'being tough';
- wanting to invest time in a private life while feeling pressured to commit time and energy to work;
- experiencing differences between their 'own and others' orientations regarding learning to teach.

These clearly indicate that beginning teachers are trying to establish their identity in this new professional sphere, balancing the desire to fulfil what is expected while reconciling some of their own views and experiences with the new role. As previously mentioned, a useful coping strategy employed by the teachers was found to be seeking support from a *significant other* usually a mentor or trusted colleague along with *searching for a solution yourself*. In the research, some recognised that they just needed to put up with the situation and this usually related to trainees wanting to take on more responsibility along with ensuring they successfully passed their placement or achieved Qualified Teacher Status (QTS). As a trainee there needs to be a recognition that there are criteria to be met and certain expectations to be fulfilled in order to qualify and although these may not sit easily always with personal or professional views, a pragmatic approach needs to be taken in order to succeed. Glazzard (2016, p. 306) gives very practical advice on the need to 'quickly learn the "rules" of being a teacher if you want to be treated as an equal and valued member of the profession' and this aligns with a lot of other work on how teachers in the early stages see their primary goal as blending in and being enculturated into their new environment (Day et al., 2006a).

Learning the procedures and practices and aligning these with your own values and beliefs is something that can be challenging and for many teachers does become easier as they progress in their career, build confidence and become more assured of their own methods and views. After a few years, most teachers' views are beginning to change and they are much more confident in challenging and questioning what they believed and what they see going on around them. This should be viewed as a positive thing as it shows a willingness to question and reflect, but this should always be underpinned by evidence and understanding of others' views. Key to this will be supportive mentoring during induction and throughout the early stages to enable purposeful discussions and new ways of working to be explored, tested and evaluated fully. These in turn will help to build the professional identity and enable the beginning teacher to assimilate the experiences and, in some cases, cope with the tensions they feel.

Part of this process will be reflection and this is well-known as a vital skill for the teacher at all stages of their career. The practice of reflection is well-documented by writers such as Kolb and Schon with an emphasis on the cyclical nature of the process and the need for action and change as a result of reflection. Ghaye's model (2011, p. 31) is particularly relevant in the context of professional identity as he identifies four foci for reflection on practice which are helpful here:

- **Reflection on values:** self – others – action.
- **Reflection on practice:** political – professional – personal.
- **Reflection on improvement:** construction – interpretation – validation.
- **Reflection on context:** partnership – culture – empowerment.

Using these as foci should enable us to reflect more comprehensively on the different elements that influence the formation and development of the professional identity. Taking us back to where we started, it helps us to consider perhaps how our values have changed or shifted in the light of the contexts in which we have worked, the people we have worked with and the political and social changes that are constantly occurring.

Pause to reflect

Thinking back over your teaching career so far

- What remains consistent in your approaches and views of teaching and learning and what is changing or evolving?
- How is your practice developing in the light of experience, new initiatives and challenging situations? Can you identify a specific example of how your practice or views have changed in relation to each of these?
- How are you balancing personal and professional roles and how are these aligning or perhaps even separating?

Case study: comments from an experienced member of a senior leadership team on 'Have you been able to hold onto your values as a teacher?'

I have been a primary school teacher for more than 30 years and have undertaken many roles in schools. I have worked through a time of ever-changing curriculums and increasing testing regimes. However, I have always loved my job and aimed to hold onto my core values. I love working with children as they surprise and delight me daily. I start the year with my new class collaboratively setting up our class rules so that they have ownership and feel part of the process. One of our rules is always about mutual respect. Once you have gained the children's trust and respect, your classroom is a happy place. I have maintained my sense of humour and children love being able to laugh with you. One of my main principles is to continue to be creative and inspiring. After so many years it would be easy to fall back on pre-prepared work but I only do this if it is relevant and effective. I would rather create a new, interactive session that excites me as much as it does the children. I am always learning new approaches and facts and I still love to learn from other, much younger, staff. It is possible to hold onto your values. There are times when you are challenged and frustrated by paperwork and by initiatives, but there are ways to make most learning fun and interesting.

It is important that teachers maintain their own individuality and hold on to their values and to the reasons that they first entered this profession, but also change and adapt as they mature and develop and experience different contexts. Professional identity is not a stable entity and that openness to new opportunities and experiences, to be willing to challenge, question and reflect will enable a strong identity to develop. 'Teachers' sense of a positive professional identity is associated with well-being and job satisfaction and is a key factor in their effectiveness' (Day et al., 2006b). Further chapters in this book will explore ways to maintain creativity and to develop personal resilience.

Chapter summary

It is important to form your own professional identity and teaching is very worthwhile if you are able to align your personal and professional identities. Clearly, as a teacher you never stop learning; you continue to develop your own craft, reacting and adapting to classroom events. It is important to work collaboratively with colleagues as this forms a supportive network. It is imperative that teachers understand, acknowledge and expect that they will encounter professional tensions, and that this is normal. Teachers must be willing to question, reflect and adapt.

References

Alexander, R. (ed.) (2010) *Children, Their World, Their Education: Final Report and Recommendations of the Cambridge Primary Review*. London: Routledge.

Ball, S.J. (2003) The teacher's soul and the terrors of performativity. *Journal of Educational Policy*, 18(2), 215-228.

Blatchford, R. (2015) *The Teachers' Standards in the Classroom*. London: Sage.

Carroll, J. & Alexander, G. (2016) *The Teachers' Standards in Primary Schools*. London: Sage.

Claxton, G., Chambers, M., Powell, G. & Lucas, B. (2012) *The Learning Powered School*. Bristol: TLO.

Coe, R., Aloisi, C., Higgins, S. & Elliot Major, L. (2014) *What Makes Great Teaching? Review of Underpinning Research*. Available at www.suttontrust.com/wp-content/uploads/2014/10/What-Makes-Great-Teaching-REPORT.pdf.

Cooper, P. & McIntyre, D. (1996) *Effective Teaching and Learning: Teachers' and Students' Perspectives*. Maidenhead: Open University Press.

Cushman, P. & Cowan, J. (2010) Enhancing student self-worth in the primary learning environment: teachers' views and students' views. *Pastoral Care in Education*, 28(2), 81–95.

Day, C., Kington A., Stobart, G. & Sammons, P. (2006a) The personal and professional selves of teachers: stable and unstable identities. *British Educational Research Journal*, 32(4), 601–616.

Day, C., Stobart, G., Sammons, P., Kington, A., Gu, Q., Smees, R. & Mujtaba, T. (2006b) *Variations in Teachers' Work, Lives and Effectiveness*. London: DfES Research Report 743.

DfE (2012) Teachers' Standards. Available at www.gov.uk/government/publications/teachers-standards.

Dweck, C.S. (2008) *Mindset: The New Psychology of Success*. New York: Random House.

Eaude, T. (2012) *How Do Expert Primary Classteachers Really Work?* Northwich: Critical Publishing Ltd.

General Teaching Council for Northern Ireland (2011) www.gtcni.org.uk.

General Teaching Council for Scotland (2012) www.gtcs.org.uk.

Gerver, R. (2012) *Creating Tomorrow's Schools Today*. London: Bloomsbury.

Ghaye, T. (2011) *Teaching and Learning through Reflective Practice*, 2nd ed. Abingdon: Routledge.

Glazzard, J. (2016) *Learning to be an Outstanding Primary Teacher*. Northwich: Critical Publishing.

Goodman, J. (2009) Respect-due and respect-earned: negotiating student-teacher relationships. *Ethics and Education*, 4(1), 3–17.

Goodson, I. (2000) The principled professional. *Prospects*, 30(2), 182–188.

Gu, Q. (2014) Being a teacher in times of change, in A. Pollard (ed.), *Readings for Reflective Teaching in Schools*. London: Bloomsbury.

Hattie, J. (2012) *Visible Learning for Teachers: Maximising Impact on Learning*. London: Routledge.

Livingston, K. & Di Nardo, P. (2016) Becoming a teacher, in D. Wyse & S. Rogers (ed.), *A Guide to Early Years and Primary Teaching*. London: Sage.

Muijs, D. & Reynolds, D. (2011) *Effective Teaching: Evidence and Practice*. London: Sage.

Nias, J. (1989) *Primary Teachers Talking*. London: Routledge.

Pillen, M., Beijaard, D. & den Brok, P. (2013) Tensions in beginning teachers' professional identity development, accompanying feelings and coping strategies. *European Journal of Teacher Education*, 36(3), 240–260.

Polesel, J. (2014) Impact of high stakes testing. *Journal of Education Policy*, 29(5), 640–657.

Pollard, A. (2014) *Reflective Teaching*, 3rd ed. London: Continuum.

Shulman, L.S. (2004) *The Wisdom of Practice- Essay on Teaching, Learning and Learning to Teach*. San Francisco: Jossey Bass.

Standards for Registration Education Workforce Council for Wales (n.d.) www.ewc.wales/site/index.php/en/fitness-to-practise/code-of-professional-conduct-and-practice-pdf/file.

Teaching Council Ireland (2016) www.teachingcouncil.ie/en.

Tröhler, T. (2017) The paradox of being a teacher. ResearchGate. Accessed at www.researchgate.net/publication/312014457_The_Paradox_of_Being_a_Teacher.

Troman, G. (2008) Primary teacher identity, commitment and career in performative school cultures. *British Educational Research Journal*, 34(5), 619–633.

PART II

Challenges facing the professional

4 The global professional – educational futures in the making?

Sue Wayman

Introduction

Globalisation raises, for professional teachers, new questions of educational purpose and responsibility. The processes and outcomes of globalisation are complex and contested, but generally there is some measure of consensus that, driven by technological developments in transport, communication and resource use, there has been increased movement of goods, ideas, people and issues around the world.

Harvey (1990) talks of socio-cultural changes involving 'time-space compression' through information and communication technologies; others of systemic, interconnected and interdependent changes between economic, political, socio-cultural, psychological and environmental realms of analysis (Held, McGrew, Goldblatt & Perraton, 1999; Lechner, 2009; Ritzer, 2010). In general, all such discussions raise concerns of social justice and increasingly of sustainability, which emphasises intergenerational as well as international principles and educational purposes worthy of consideration.

> **By the end of the chapter you will:**
> * Understand notions of the global professional within education.
> * Explore debates surrounding globalisation and the implications for practice.
> * Consider cultural diversity in educational practice.
> * Understand what we mean by the global classroom (Pike & Selby, 1999, 2000).

Globalisation

The historical and current processes of globalisation – and the way we talk about such processes and change – have, in many ways, reconfigured our professional practices and responsibilities as professional teachers now and for the future (Goodson & Rudd, 2016; Vulliamy, 2010). For many, globalisation involves systemic and interconnected changes within and between economic, political, socio-cultural and environmental realms of analysis (Held et al., 1999; Lechner, 2009; Ritzer, 2010).

Pause to reflect

- Consider all the ways in which you are 'connected' to the world – lifestyle, travel, communication, etc. In what ways do these connections (you may want to pick one) link to the economic, political, socio-cultural and environmental 'realms of analysis'?
- What are your main sources of information about the world?
- What are the dominant stories about our connections with the world that you read, hear or tell?
- What are the key global issues that you know/care about?

Globalisation is often discussed in relation to the greater interconnectedness of the world, and to the 'diverse mobilities of peoples, objects, images, information and wastes' (Urry, 2000, p. 185). Economic and political competition within a world market has, for many, been furthered by international governmental organisations (IGOs) such as the World Trade Organization, the International Monetary Fund, the World Bank and the Organisation for Economic Co-operation and Development (Akkari & Dassen, 2008; Torabian, 2014). Global change has been driven by neoliberal ideologies that stress free market consumer interaction dominated by transnational corporations, and technological advances in transport and communication technologies. Held et al. (1999, p. 2) note the systemic nature of globalisation, involving the 'widening, deepening and speeding up of worldwide interconnectedness in all aspects of contemporary social life, from the cultural to the criminal, the financial to the spiritual'. Robertson suggests that 'globalisation as a concept refers both to the compression of the world and the intensification of consciousness of the world as a whole' (1992, p. 8). In this is the suggestion that globalisation is an embodied agentic phenomenon (Hill, 2014) as much as it is a structural one, it progresses through individual and local (refr)action and agency grounded in a wider global context (Goodson & Rudd, 2016) as will be discussed in the next section.

Benefits and issues with globalisation

Held et al. (1999; Mackay, 2000) suggest there are different perspectives on the benefits and issues associated with globalisation with 'sceptics' denying, in various ways and to various degrees, that this is a phenomenon at all.

For the authors, *hyperglobalists* are those who believe that globalisation is a feature of history and contemporary life promoting profound change in global relations with equally profound implications for the future. For some hyperglobalists, usually in businesses or governments, this is seen as positive in terms of neoliberal marketisation and notions of competitive and comparative advantage, often furthered through education (Selby, 1999, 2005).

Critical hyperglobalists, often marginalised by the processes of globalisation, or advocating for those marginalised, present a range of neo-Marxist and other critical challenges to capitalist accumulation that reinforce and extend inequality and environmental damage. From this perspective, globalisation has promoted or exacerbated local as well as global experiences of connectivity and interdependence but also inequality, complexity, uncertainty and risk (Beck, 1992; Hargreaves, 2003; Selby, 2005; Claxton & Lucas, 2009; Noddings, 2010; Yang & Valdés-Cotera, 2011). According to Held et al. (1999) others hold more *transformational* views, challenging the idea that the processes and outcomes of globalisation are known, or structurally determined and perhaps, therefore, the future is open to change. While borne out of critique of the global *status quo*, this potentially emphasises a more hopeful view of the part we all can play, through our professional agency, in creating a better world.

Pause to reflect

Look back at your thoughts from the first set of reflective questions. Where do you sit in relation to the perspectives on globalisation?

- Do you embrace the new challenges or are you more sceptical?
- Can you see how globalisation can create new opportunities for educators?
- What sources of evidence might you access to help inform your decisions?

Globalised political ideologies and associated policies have had indirect but still profound effects on teaching, learning and teacher professionalism (Hargreaves, 2000; Vidovich, 2006; Torabian, 2014). Torabian suggests this has had its roots in neoliberal and competitive market worldviews and economically driven change in educational spaces in terms of content, structure, accessibility and outcomes. International comparison and competition – via, for example, PISA, TIMSS, PIRLs – have been used by governments to inform national policy, alongside other forms of policy 'travelling' and 'borrowing' (Vidovich, 2006; Vulliamy, 2010; Biesta, 2011). An example of this would be the No Child Left Behind policy initiative in the USA that we in England borrowed as Every Child Matters (Robinson, 2014). Seddon et al. (2013, cited in Schweisfurth, 2013, p. 173) note: 'In the contemporary education policy milieu, ideas of all kinds are constantly being transferred, translated and transformed across national and other boundaries.' Our responses to globalisation and associated educational policies may be varied and complex. For Goodson and Rudd (2016, p. 6) 'institutional, collective and individual responses will vary significantly, ranging from compliant integration, contestation and resistance, through to decoupling'. It is suggested by the authors that in England the tendency has been compliant integration.

Globalisation as a catalyst for changes in how we view the world

Changes in policy offer new ideas, benchmarks of professional accountability, and normative calls to action that, as noted, teachers will embrace, resist or reframe. Ultimately, how we translate, transform and enact the flow of ideas associated with globalisation and educational perspectives comes down to choice and our sense of agency. 'The future directions of global society depend on us as ordinary world citizens, on what moral positions we choose and what battles we are prepared to fight' (Cohen & Kennedy, 2012, p. 406). As such, our personal understandings of, engagement with and commitment to tackling the issues seen by many as emergent from globalisation will be key in shaping our professional practices.

Informing our thinking about being a global professional, normative concerns that lie central to notions of teacher professionalism have increasingly been shaped by global as well as national and local policy and ideas, while at the same time being influential in shaping, sharing and enacting globalised academic and professional practitioner responses. These have come about, in no small measure, due to the conscious transformational efforts of individuals and groups within and beyond the education system who still believe the path to the future is not set. In times of rapid change, a new era of instability, innovation and contradiction sits alongside older patterns of organisation and practice in education. Dominant discourses of 'modernity' have historically celebrated human privilege, progress and technological innovation, and in this contributed to a society largely complacent about social and ecological exploitation;

> Emerging within this attitude of superiority and exploitation are very powerful beliefs that govern public, industrial and frequently personal decisions. Economism, progressivism, industrialism, consumerism and individualism serve to set the direction of human actions.
>
> (Coates and Leahy, 2006, p. 3)

Postmodernism, on the other hand, for Edwards and Usher (2000) offers a way of understanding the changes and ethical pluralism that globalisation has increasingly engendered. This resonates for some a different notion of professionalism in contemporary educational practice and research. Hargreaves conceptualises this postmodern context as one 'where teachers deal with a diverse and complex clientele, in conditions of increasing moral uncertainty, where many methods of approach are possible, and where more and more social groups have an influence and a say' (Hargreaves, 2000, p. 231). The complexity, diversity and inherent pluralism of ideas and values in education has 'muddied the waters' in terms of epistemic and moral consensus or authority, and this for educators can create an uncomfortable uncertainty in their daily practices.

Pause to reflect

How has globalisation changed what you do in your classroom? Have the changes that you have made led to a greater understanding of different ideas and perspectives? Have you had to rethink any aspects of your pedagogy to cater for different cultural backgrounds?

Carneiro (2011, p. 3), taking in the modern/postmodern, structure/agency arguments, suggests that contemporary education sits 'on the thin borderline between stability and change, between preservation and innovation'. Higher education is also considered to be 'caught between two trends' where dominant and naturalised –hegemonic – ideas and actions strengthen 'the industrial society model of fragmentation, prescription, management, control and accountability' with an alternative if 'marginal trend is based on integration, self-determination, agency, learning and reflexivity' (Unterhalter & Carpentier, 2010, cited in Peters & Wals, 2013, p. 86). This thin borderline throws into question the purpose, form and function of education for the future (Biesta, 2011). For Claxton and Lucas, within the context of lifelong learning uncertainty abounds:

> The health of individuals, communities and societies depends on the encouragement of learning that may not look valuable in the light of immediate or short-term needs. It is not just entrepreneurial, technical or vocational skills that need supporting, nor the abilities to navigate the internet and check Wikipedia entries. In the next 50 years, the knowledge that our society needs may as likely come from developments in the arts, spirituality or philosophy as from the invention of ever cleverer machines. We don't know. All we can say, with any confidence, is that lifelong learning, in this broad and intelligent sense, is a vital investment for individuals, communities, nations, and ultimately the planet.
>
> (Claxton & Lucas, 2009, p. 8)

Pause to reflect

What knowledge, skills and attributes do you think it will be important to hold, teach or foster in students to become 'lifelong learners'?

Being a global professional: global, lifelong and reflexive learning

The emphasis in discourses of modernity, of economic man, progress, indus-trialisation, consumerism and individualism have become, for critics, part of the 'western mindset' (Jackson, 2003, cited in Wals & Jickling, 2002). For Mezirow (2000, p. 138) this mind-set is hegemonic in nature, a 'conspiracy of the normal', where despite our sense that we are working to make life easier for ourselves, 'the dark irony of hegemony is that educators take pride in acting on the very assumptions that work to entrap them... [we] become willing prisoners who lock their own cell doors behind them'. Thus hegemony is an important concept in ideological critique (Brookfield, 1987, 2005), involving what Hicks (2004) calls *rule by consent*. Education has felt as well as having been implicated in the hegemonic pressures of globalisation, as noted, where we 'directly experience the risks, uncertainties and pressures of working and living within a globalized, weightless knowledge economy' (Blewitt, 2004, p. 11).

Beck (1992) suggests that such processes has led to the 'disempowerment of our senses related to the risks generated by our industrial and techno-logical development', and to new levels of self-critique or 'reflexive mod-ernity'. The author notes that this has, in the individual, heightened 'identity risks' with a fragmentation of alliances socially, spatially and temporally. Risk presupposes, as did Bakhtin (1986), ideas of choice, calculability and respon-sibility, and whether the future is regarded as fixed and inevitable or as a sub-ject of human agency. Beck's optimism for 'private reflexivity [as the] prior basis for more public forms' (1992, p. 7), can only come about, he suggests, if one takes account of the more situated understandings that people have of the world and their place in it so as to transform their understandings and ability to act.

> Transformative learning is learning that transforms problematic frames of reference –sets of fixed assumptions and expectations (habits of mind, meaning perspectives, mindsets) – to make them more inclusive, discrim-inating, open, reflective, and emotionally able to change. Such frames of reference are better than others because they are more likely to generate beliefs and opinions that will prove more true or justified to guide action.
> (Mezirow, 2000, pp. 58-59)

He suggests that this involves 'a willingness to construe knowledge and values from multiple perspectives without loss of commitment to one's own values' (Mezirow, 2000, pp.12–13). For Sterling (2011), transformation involves experience of challenges and threats to existing beliefs and ideas which may involve resistance and perturbation:

> Epistemic learning can be deeply uncomfortable, because it involves a restructuring of basic assumptions caused by the recognition of 'incoherence' between assumptions and experience. This crisis experience can be traumatic – although for some it is inspiring – and can be a lengthy process over time as mental models undergo radical change.
>
> (Sterling & Baines, 2002, cited in Sterling, 2011, p. 25)

Challenges prompted by the incoherence between assumptions and experience may in part link to the multiple demands made of us as professionals.

Teaching as a paradoxical profession

Hargreaves and Lo (2000, p.173) suggest that in recent times teaching has increasingly become 'the paradoxical profession'. For the authors, while teachers and schools are the catalysts of change in the informational society, they are also its casualties – 'casualties of the weakening of the welfare safety net, casualties of reduced expenditure on the public good, casualties of the students' families caught in social upheaval, casualties of the widespread decommitment to public life'. They go on to suggest that we teach in times of 'deprofessionalisation' where declining support, limited pay, restricted opportunities to learn from colleagues, work overload and standardisation limit opportunities for alternative views of curriculum and pedagogy to emerge.

Sellars (2017) suggests that professionalism is a social construction and is thus historically, geographically and culturally mediated. This involves what has been termed globalisation (Robertson, 1992) or refraction (Goodson & Rudd, 2016), where diverse local interpretations and enactments of global structural forces are possible and increasingly evident. The inherent and ongoing pluralism is, for Sellars, important if we are to engage in the critical discussion and educational transformations that can perhaps help us respond and promote more socially just and sustainable change. An issue, it is suggested, is that we in hegemonic compliance to standards, performativity, accountability, the imposition of the mandatory curriculum and predetermined pedagogical approaches, are failing to question the purposes of education as noted by Biesta (2011) above.

Questions of educational purpose and practice have long held sway in discourses of professionalism. Schön (1998) saw the concept of professional teaching practice as significantly different from other working contexts.

Using Hughes' (1959) idea of the professional as 'one who makes a claim to extraordinary knowledge in matters of great human importance' and Dewey's (1933) notion of 'traditions of calling' (cited in Schön, 1998, p. 32), he defined professions as having an 'appreciative system' of shared values, preferences, norms and conventions of action, institutional settings, and units of activity which constitute acceptable professional conduct (p. 33). For Altrichter, in a similar voice '[f]ull professionalism of teachers involves the competence to interweave practical action and reflection on it in such a way that action is moral, intellectual and practical' (Altrichter, 2005, p. 12). Hoyle (1980, cited in Craft, 2000, p. 198), drew on the language of the restricted professional who could be differentiated from, and become, the extended professional. While restricted professionals learning was 'intuitive, classroom-focused and based on experience rather than theory', the extended professional would seek to locate their teaching practice in its broader educational context, and would engage in collaborative and systemic evaluation in the belief that through such research and development activities, practice could be improved.

Being a professional is, according to others (Beaty, 1997; Sellars, 2017), an attitude to work that goes beyond knowledge and skills. More experience, Beaty suggests, does not guarantee more learning if we become complacent. In a time of globalisation, complexity and change, a transformational, continual and self-directed form of learning has been promoted as a means of meeting the challenges that this presents (Askew & Carnell, 1998). This, according to the authors, embodies the principles of meta-learning, holistic learning incorporating autobiography and reflection to help 'challenge the thinking about events, circumstances and philosophies which constitute and value the status quo' (Knowles, 1993, cited in Askew & Carnell, 1998, p. 157). It is through committed critical reflection on our practice that perceived problems relating to the educational context can be identified, illuminated through educational and wider theory and provide a basis for critically informed action or *praxis* (Beaty, 1997; Kemmis, 1993; Sellars, 2017). Reflection, however, is a difficult undertaking in isolation (Kuit, Reay & Freeman, 2001, p. 139), and this necessitates a collaborative approach to evaluation and learning.

According to Doherty and Jarvis (2016, p. 219) there are nine characteristics of professional development that may be important organisationally. Professional development:

- Begins with an end in mind.
- Challenges thinking and changes practice.
- Based on assessment of individual and school needs.
- Involves connecting theory and practice.
- Involves varied, rich and sustainable learning opportunities.
- Uses action research and enquiry as key tools.

- Is enhanced through collaboration in learning and practice.
- Is enhanced by creating Professional Learning Communities within and beyond schools.
- Requires leadership that create the necessary conditions.

Features or principles of a good professional have for Goodson (2000) been grounded in notions of active care, collaborative cultures and continuous (or lifelong) learning. In many ways, the list reflects and reverberates into other suggested ethical considerations of professional agency (Sellars, 2017). In a globalised world, however, there are, given the socially constructed and relativist nature of professionalism mentioned, potential issues of creating a discourse that furthers cultural imperialism or colonisation of the individual through the promotion of 'ideal types' relating to teachers as professionals that position us in terms of our place in the system. As Gaudelli and Ousley (2009, cited in Czerniawski, 2011, p.171) suggest this does not account for and perhaps undermines the idiosyncratic, creative nature of people and potential for positive change. It also tends toward the assumption of single paths to professionalism when it can hold both utilitarian and humanitarian aspects, or as Edwards (1997) notes, be shaped by our entrepreneurial, professional and activist selves where we try to keep our jobs, maintain the traditions on which our jobs are based, and yet at the same time change the system of which we are often the beneficiaries. In calls for global thinking, there has also been increased emphasis on local action, participation and heterogeneity of ideas (Turner, 2005, p.58), to the extent that global issues are clearly linked to local solutions, and changes at the micro-level of opinions, attitudes and behaviour.

Being a global professional for many means being or becoming a lifelong learner, and promoting lifelong learning through our curriculum and pedagogy (Helterbran, 2005). For Yang & Valdés-Cotera:

> We are now living in a fast-changing and complex social, economic and political world to which we need to adapt by increasingly rapidly acquiring new knowledge, skills and attitudes in a wide range of contexts. An individual will not be able to meet life challenges unless he or she becomes a lifelong learner, and a society will not be sustainable unless it becomes a learning society. Furthermore, equal access to learning opportunities is an indispensable condition to realise the right to education for all. In response to these needs, lifelong learning has become a guiding principle of education development and reform worldwide.
>
> (Yang & Valdés-Cotera, 2011, p. v)

In this global context, and in consideration of the critiques of 'ideal types' noted above, we are also called on to become agents of change (Goodson, 2000; Vandeyar, 2017). Vandeyar draws on Fullan (2001, in Vandeyar, 2017,

pp.376–377) to suggest this may come about locally through changes in practice along three dimensions:

- Using revised material and instructional resources in the curriculum.
- Considering and using new teaching approaches.
- Possibly altering our beliefs, pedagogical assumptions and critical understanding of theories underpinning new policies and programmes – as the foundation for lasting reform.

Pause to reflect

Looking at Fullan's points above, how have you adapted your practice
for an increasingly pluralist society?

Developing agency as a principled professional

Agency for Newman and Dale (2005, p. 482) 'is necessary for citizens to be
able to adapt to their sociocultural environment, and more importantly to
respond and transcend tragedy and crisis'. Links have thus been made to
notions of agency and post or reflexive modernity, where agency becomes
both more necessary and difficult to achieve, bound up as it is in a web
of alternative ways of seeing and 'part of a reflective process connecting
personal and social change' (Giddens, 1991, p. 32).

In Sen's 'capability approach' to globalisation and development, attempts
have been made to challenge the emphasis on dominant human capital
approaches to include broader notions of human flourishing, dignity and
agency (Walker, 2012). In the context of sustainability, Sen emphasises the
need to see ourselves and others as agents of change:

> we also have to go beyond the role of human beings specifically as 'con-
> sumers' or as 'people with needs', and consider, more broadly, their gen-
> eral role as agents of change who can – given the opportunity – think,
> assess, evaluate, resolve, inspire, agitate, and, through these means,
> reshape the world.
>
> (Sen, 2013, p. 7)

While wellbeing for Sen (2007) may be achieved through 'functionings'
(actions) that may show concern for others' wellbeing, his notion of agency
involves a sense of commitment to support other individuals regardless, and
perhaps at the expense of one's own wellbeing. He notes '[s]ince people are
the ultimate "agents" of change, much must depend on their inspiration and
commitment' (Sen, 2013, p. 9). Agency for Sen (2007, p. 275) 'encompasses

the goals that a person has reasons to adopt, which can *inter alia* include goals other than the advancement of his or her own well-being'. He suggests therefore a need to consider the 'extent of freedom (and the real capability to do – or achieve – what one has reason to value)' (Sen, 2013, p. 11) where a distinction between personal values, and the reason to value involves wider conceptions of the good. As such, agency becomes an assessment of 'what a person can do in line with his or her conception of the good' and the possible (Sen, 1985, cited in Alkire, 2008, p. 3). Sen (2013, p. 17) notes, how-ever, drawing on earlier work (1999): 'It has to be borne in mind that quite often the isolated individual has very little opportunity of going against established patterns of behaviour and socially accepted norms.' For Alkire (2008), drawing on Ryan and Deci (2004, in Alkire, 2008, pp. 3-4), not being able to exert agency can lead to alienation, openness to coercion, submis-sion and passivity. In essence, a lack of agency can diminish an individual's ability to flourish.

For Ahearn too, agency involves 'the socioculturally mediated capacity to act' (2001, p. 112; Emirbayer and Mische, 1998; Biesta & Tedder, 2006). It is therefore problematic to view agency as a synonym for free will or resist-ance that potentially neglects 'the social nature of agency and the pervasive influence of culture on human intentions, beliefs, and actions' (Ahearn, 2001, p. 114). It is equally problematic to succumb to 'romance of resistance', which, for the author, could neglect that agent's motivations 'are always complex and contradictory' (p. 116).

Biesta and Tedder (2006) note that the concept of agency lies at the heart of education across traditions/ideologies whether liberal, humanist or critical and emancipatory. Agency's discursive links to concepts of freedom, rational autonomy, conscientisation and moral autonomy have their home in 'modern' ideas and the authors draw on Kant's (1784, in Biesta & Tedder, 2007) definition of Enlightenment as 'man's [sic] release from his self-incurred tutelage'. Tutelage, for the author, represents 'man's inability to make use of his understanding without direction from another' (Biesta & Tedder, 2006, p. 4). They go on to suggest that there is a difference between a normative and empirical interest in agency, with the former emphasising the need for learning 'particular things' to become more agentic, and the latter recognising that agency is thrust upon us, we have the capacity of agency through processes of individualisation (Bauman, 2000; Elliott, 2002; Beck, 1992), with greater uncertainty, therefore, of what learning is needed.

Emirbayer and Mische (1998, p. 963; Biesta & Tedder, 2006) suggest agency is a 'temporally embedded process of social engagement, informed by the past, (in its habitual aspect), but also oriented toward the future (as a capacity to imagine alternative possibilities) and toward the present (as a capacity to contextualise past habits and future projects with the contingencies of the moment)', linking this concept to storylines and narratives, of refractive actions (Goodson & Rudd, 2016).

What path or form such change takes is difficult to prescribe without falling into the same traps of ethnocentrism, paternalism or indoctrination we may challenge through our critiques of the educational *status quo*. It links more to our engagement with such philosophical and ideological positions and to 'personal and internal commitment or ownership' (Goodson, 2001, cited in Vandeyar, 2017, p. 385) set within local and global collegial and collaborative communities of practice.

Pause to reflect

Consider the word 'commitment' noted by Sen (2013) above, which Trigg (1973, cited in Hill, 2014, p. 298) defines as 'acting in accordance with a belief'.

- What beliefs do you hold about the purposes and processes of education?
- Given the above discussion and your own understanding, what barriers are there in our 'paradoxical profession' that may hinder acting in accordance to your beliefs?

Beliefs and values, according to Hill (2014, p. 298), are inextricably linked with values being 'the priorities which individuals and societies attach to certain beliefs, experiences, and objects, in deciding how they shall live and what they shall treasure'. The author suggests, however, that we often hold conflicting values in relation to our beliefs, which can generate paralysis or moral dilemmas. Our previous acculturation may also shade our views of the importance of particular values, and we may be subject to external compulsions that silence us and deny agency, or we may lack the will to act without consideration of the wider good. Perhaps the findings by Hill that students applied their values inconsistently in different situations over time, highlights the problematic nature of calls for active professional agency associated with globalisation. However, we should not forget the normative calls that globalisation has engendered in terms of rights, social justice and sustainability, which potentially can inspire us: 'We can learn to reflect critically on the particular discourses that surround us and we can intervene in discourses that we believe are problematic. Through conscious commitment and effort, we can change the discourses that surround us, over time' (Karlberg, 2008, p. 311). Selby (2005) notes that the policies that dominate education in a global competitive knowledge economy and employment market embrace wider discourses of development (as neoliberal

Table 4.1 Global education[s] and relations to the global economy (adapted from Selby, 1999, 2005)

Global competitiveness education	Reformist global education	Transformative global education
To equip the learner with competencies for engagement in global society and the global marketplace.	Liberal appreciation of other cultures.	Explicitly and rigorously ethical.
Embraces globalisation	Over-concentration on notion of interdependence – superficial embracement.	Mutual embedding of individual and social transformation.
Emphasises education for economic development and social cohesion.	Management interpretation of how to deal with the disequilibria of interdependence and the deleterious effects of globalisation.	Solidarity with struggles for justice, dignity and freedom.
Strong emphasis on knowledge, skills and qualifications.		Confronts structural violence.
	Uncritical assumptions about the inexorability of human progress.	Stresses ecological security.
De-emphasises values.		Conscientising and empowering pedagogy.
	Embrace values directed towards tampering with rather than turning round the global system.	In its biocentric expression, decentres the human project.

globalisation), at the expense of questions of values and criticism of the global condition, whether economic, social or environmental.

It is suggested that dominant political and educational ideologies and curriculum models are linked to technical instrumentalism, rationality and neo-conservative traditionalism (Young, 1998). Habermas (1972) famously suggested that seeking knowledge always serves certain interests. These he defined as technical interests of generalisation, prediction and control; practical (communicative) interests involving the hermeneutical understanding and interpretation of humans; and emancipatory interests that sought freedom from the fetters of the past, of culture and our own alienation.

Kemmis, Cole & Suggett (1983) speak in similar, if more general terms, of the classification of education as vocational/neoclassical, liberal progressive and socially critical. Similar models of adjectival educations in relationship with the dominant orders of systems have been presented in relation to global education (Selby, 2005).

Political globalisation has seen the rise or reaffirmation of certain principles echoed in the table above which are legally and morally influential in our practices as a global professional for example to be inclusive and promote social justice (Goodson & Rudd, 2016). The two principles chosen here are linked by Carneiro (2011) to discourses of lifelong learning The first principle is inclusion linked to human, and children's rights. For Ife (2008, p. 1):

> Human rights represent one of the most powerful ideas in contemporary discourse. In a world of economic globalisation, where individualism, greed and becoming rich are seen as the most important things in life, and where at the same time the formerly secure moral positions for judging our actions seem to be declining into the morass of postmodern relativism, the idea of human rights provides an alternative moral reference point for those who would seek to reaffirm the values of humanity.

In relation to children's rights, the UNCRC (1989) reaffirmed global and national commitments to protection of and provision for children. For the first time, however, children's civil and political rights were recognised, and ideas of children 'having a say' in the services they receive became enshrined in, for example, Schools: Achieving Success (DfES, 2001) and Every Child Matters (DfES, 2004), although again we need to remember that policy will not translate into action unless we, as teachers, actively promote, and listen to, their voice.

The second principle is sustainable development, which for some is a liberal reformist ideal and globalised policy prescription that, while still economically driven, brings ideas and measures of social equality, and environmental quality into 'development' thinking and (educational) practice, providing a 'triple bottom line' by which we should evaluate change (Dawe, Jucker & Martin, 2005; Blewitt, 2004). Education for Sustainable Development (ESD) is part of a globalised policy discourse (Sterling, 2004; Wals, 2012), which culminated in the United Nations Decade of Education for Sustainable Development (DESD, UNESCO - 2005-2014). The DESD stressed the centrality of individual, cultural and global values in this endeavour:

> Understanding your own values, the values of the society you live in and the values of others around the world is a central part of educating for a sustainable future. Each nation, cultural group and individual must learn the skills of recognising their own values and assessing these values in the context of sustainability.
>
> (UNESCO, 2005, p. 3)

In international governance and policy development, the Brundtland Report *Our Common Future* (WCED, 1987) was pivotal in both defining sustainable development (SD), and in partly shaping subsequent political and environmental discourses that surround its globalised educational policy prescriptions. The often-cited definition of SD was optimistic in the ability of national governments and local communities to manage environmental threats and meet 'basic' needs: 'Humanity has the ability to make development sustainable – to ensure that it meets the needs of the present without compromising the ability for future generations to meet their own needs' (WCED, 1987, p. 8). The WCED warned, however, rather as Beck (1992) had, that our knowledge and technical abilities were insufficient to address social and environmental issues and that 'the rate of change is outstripping the ability of scientific disciplines and our current capabilities to assess and advise' (WCED, 1987, p. 22/243). This, it was suggested, warranted 'break[ing] out of past patterns', where 'security must be sought through change' (p. 22/243). Ongoing calls for change will now be examined in light of a particular issue in and surrounding contemporary education, that of cultural diversity, prejudice and the implications for global professional practice.

Being a global professional: working with diversity

Globalisation 'involves considerable increase in global, including "local", complexity and density' (Robertson, 1992, p. 188). Globalisation has changed school demographics, increasing diversity in the classroom. According to the DfE (2011), about a quarter of school pupils are from an ethnic minority, and it is this focus on culture and ethnicity that will be the focus of this section. Reynolds and Vinterek (2013) suggest that as a result of global changes, our practice is situated in hybrid classrooms, where students have access to a range of global information and perspectives, demanding greater responsiveness and flexibility on the part of teachers. Critics suggest that racism exists along two lines – colour and culture. The history of racism is linked to European colonialism and the growth of the slave trade, where colour was linked to notions of inferiority. Cultural racism is seen to have a more subtle but still detrimental effect in terms of performance and achievement (Curtis & Pettigrew, 2010).

Globalisation and increased interconnection has been considered as a cultural phenomenon being 'the most direct, obvious and visible way in which we experience these interconnections in our daily lives' (Mackay, 2000, p. 48). Culture, according to Cohen and Kennedy (2012, p. 34) is the 'repertoire of learned ideas, values, knowledge, aesthetic preferences, rules and customs shared by a collectivity of social actors', which links our constructions of meaning with location and circumstance. For Williams (1980, cited in Schirato & Webb, 2003), cultural meanings involve dominant, residual and emergent worldviews, beliefs and values. As such we need to consider culture, in the context of globalisation as a dynamic force for change as well as setting parameters for thought and action.

> **Pause to reflect**
>
> *Perspectives on cultural globalisation*
> Looking back to the perspectives on globalisation noted earlier, how do you think each would talk about cultural globalisation?
>
> - Positive hyperglobalists
> - Negative hyperglobalists
> - Sceptics
> - Transformationalists

Positive hyperglobalists according to Mackay (2000) talk of cultural change in terms of a new or emergent 'global village', where new ideas and opportunities emerge for positive change. Pessimists stress inequalities, homogenisation, Westernisation and consumption linked to inequalities of power enacted as cultural imperialism. Sceptics stress that cultural diversity is bound up in historical processes of nationalism and localism that persist today. Transformationalists stress agency and cultural change, diversity and unpredictability. The impact of globalisation in relation to culture has tended to be viewed in a pessimistic light (Tomlinson, 2003), in part through the growth of anti-immigration and xenophobic tendencies.

For those new to our schools and other educational institutions, there are issues of potential ignorance and intolerance. YouGov Research (2013, cited in Gaultner & Green, 2015) suggests that public hostility to immigration has increased in the last decade. NFER research (Keating, Kerr, Benton, Mundy & Lopes, 2010) notes similar trends in their longitudinal study with more than 24,000 English pupils aged 11 to 18. For those who perhaps are British yet identify with or are identified as belonging to different cultural groups, similar issues are evident (Keddie, 2014). This suggests an issue that is both worthy of our attention, and problematic in terms of global professional practice.

In order to promote inclusion of all children - as is their right - professionals are being called on, and no doubt through our own 'powerful ethic of care and integrity', consider it our professional responsibility to be culturally competent (Czerniawski, 2011, p. 171). For Czerniawski, this demands, in professional practice, critical self-awareness, awareness of our power and privilege and of our biases and prejudices. Reynolds (2001) says that 'it is the knowledge, beliefs and values of the teacher that are brought to bear in creating an effective learning environment for pupils, making the teacher a critical influence in education'. Emphasis on cultural explanations for student's engagement, behaviour and educational outcomes are thought to be prevalent in contemporary education and this is problematic to effective inclusion (Keddie, 2014; Gaultner & Green, 2015) and fostering wider social tolerance.

Vandeyar (2017, p. 377) draws on Bandura (1986) and Dewey (1933) to suggest that our beliefs and perceptions play a critical role in how we teach and understand diversity. These are context-specific and derive, in part, from our own process of socialisation via 'our own schooling experiences, observed classroom practices, family and community responses to diversity' that can lead to ethnocentric tendencies. Citing Spradley and McCurdy (1987) the author notes the hegemonic nature of this mind-set:

> We tend to think that the norms we follow represent the 'natural' way human beings do things. Those who behave otherwise are judged morally wrong. This viewpoint is ethnocentric, which means that people think their own culture represents the best, or at least the most appropriate way for human beings to live.
>
> (Vandeyar, 2017, p. 377)

Ethnocentrism in part is fuelled by our tendencies to think of others through lenses of biological determinism, essentialism and reductionism (Keddie, 2014). Overcoming this, demands, for Keddie, that we continually question our personal politics and the politics of education more generally, including our acts aimed at inclusion. Drawing on Freire (1993) she notes that our best efforts to include those marginalised can be described as 'false generosity' where paternalistic support can maintain existent issues of power and inequality. Exalting ethnic minorities is, according to Keddie, equally problematic in moves to inclusion in that it potentially maintains inverted dualisms where we consider minority others to be 'more "spiritual", more "interesting", more "cultural" that the supposedly shallow, monetaristic, culturally poor white majority' (McConaghy, 2000, cited in Keddie, 2014, p. 313). This has perhaps led to a tendency to focus on food, costume and customs at the expense of more critical engagement with issues of diversity and identity, or for Modood (2010, p. 1) 'steel bands, saris and samosas... black music, exotic dress and spicy food'.

Ethnic diversity following Keddie is seen as negotiated practice rather than involving fixed knowable identities, and as such requires critical situational analysis that takes into account how we advocate for marginalised groups within systems of reform, authority and power (Goodson & Rudd, 2016). Diversity and complexity of children's identities, linked to ethnicity warrant consideration if we are not to succumb to stereotypical assumptions (Keddie, 2014; Gaultner & Green, 2015). Scott (2002) suggested that our own political views tend to predispose us to particular ideas, perspectives, curricula and pedagogies within practice, aside from or often in conflict with dominant hegemonic discourses. That is not to say that we should preach rather than teach alternative visions of the future, but that we recognise, reflect and reconfigure education that can have a positive effect on individuals and the wider world both in the present and for the future. This requires us, perhaps, to be more resilient and reflexive lifelong learners, and to promote this in and through our own professional practice where '[t]he shape of the global future rests with the reflexivity of human consciousness – the capacity to think critically about why we think what we do – and then to think and act differently' (Raskin, 2008, cited in Sterling, 2011, p.19).

For Goodson and Rudd (2016, p.6) there is a need to look to opportunities for action or agency, which they describe as 'moments of refraction', linked to narrative articulations of our professional practices aimed at positive change (for example, through action research), which offer the potential to bridge and explore what Goodson (1989, p.12; Gaultner & Green, 2015) earlier referred to as 'the story of action within a theory of context'.

Goodson's (2001) emphasis on 'the centrality of the personal domain of the teacher in sustaining educational change' (cited in Vandeyar, 2017, p.385), for teachers to attend to their commitment to act, and the 'force of personal identity projects under post-modernity which seeks new integration with internal missions'. In this, the way you translate, transform and enact the ideas presented here are linked to your professional identity and agency. In her article 'Dancing with Systems', Meadows offered an overarching sentiment that could perhaps inspire you:

> The future can't be predicted, but it can be envisioned and brought lovingly into being. Systems can't be controlled, but they can be designed and redesigned. We can't surge forward with certainty into a world of no surprises, but we can expect surprises and learn from them and even profit from them. We can't impose our will upon a system. We can listen to what the system tells us, and discover how its properties and our values can work together to bring forth something much better than could ever be produced by our will alone.
>
> (Meadows, 2001)

Chapter summary

There have been a number of significant economic, political and social changes associated with globalisation that have impacted on educational curricula and practices. This has meant that the professional role and identity of the teacher has and will continue to respond to new questions of educational purpose and responsibility. Calls for paradigm change, and for teachers to extend their horizons as professionals are noted, if contested, yet they should prompt reflection by each of us as individuals, both in terms of our engagement of learners within diverse classrooms and wider globalised contexts. In this time of change, uncertainty and risk, perhaps the most evident aspect of our professional practice is working with diversity. It is suggested that we need, as professionals, to be more culturally competent and to engage in deeper and more meaningful questioning of our own, and wider, political positions, to avoid ethnocentrism or romanticism of *other* cultures.

References

Ahearn, L.A. (2001) Language and agency. *Annual Review of Anthropology*, 30, 109-137.

Akkari, A. & Dassen, P.R. (2008) *Educational Theories and Practices from the Majority World*. Thousand Oaks, CA: Sage Publications.

Alkire, S. (2008) *Concepts and Measures of Agency*. OPHI Working Paper 9: University of Oxford.

Altrichter, H. (2005) The role of the 'professional community' in action research. *Educational Action Research*, 13(1), 11-25.

Askew, W. & Carnell, E. (1998) *Transforming Learning: Individual and Global Change*. London: Cassell.

Bakhtin, M.M. (1986) *Speech Genres and Other Late Essays*. Austin, TX: University of Texas Press.

Bauman, Z. (2000) *The Individualized Society*. Cambridge: Polity Press.

Beaty, L. (1997) *Developing Your Teaching Through Reflective Practice*. Birmingham: SEDA Publications.

Beck, U. (1992) *Risk Society: Towards a New Modernity*. London: Sage.

Biesta, G.J.J. (2011) *Good Education in an Age of Measurement: Ethics, Politics, Democracy*. London: Paradigm.

Biesta, G.J.J. & Tedder, M. (2006) *How is Agency Possible? Towards an Ecological Understanding of Agency-as-Achievement*. Working paper 5. Exeter: The Learning Lives Project.

Biesta, G.J.J. & Tedder, M. (2007) Agency and learning in the lifecourse: towards an ecological perspective. *Studies in the Education of Adults*, 39(2).

Blewitt, J. (2004) Sustainability and lifelong learning, in J. Blewitt and C. Cullingford (eds.), *The Sustainability Curriculum: The Challenge for Higher Education*. London: Earthscan.

Brookfield, S.D. (1987) *Developing Critical Thinkers: Challenging Adults to Explore Alternative Ways of Thinking and Acting*. Buckingham: Open University Press.

Brookfield, S.D. (2005) *The Power of Critical Theory: Liberating Adult Learning and Teaching*. San Francisco: Jossey Bass.

Carneiro, R. (2011) Discovering the treasure of learning, in J. Yang and R. Valdés-Cotera (eds.), *Conceptual Evolution and Policy Developments in Lifelong Learning*. Hamburg: UNESCO Institute for Lifelong Learning.

Claxton, G. & Lucas, B. (2009) *School as a Foundation for Lifelong Learning: The Implications of a Lifelong Learning Perspective for the Re-Imagining of School-Age Education*. Leicester: NIACE. Available at www.niace.org.uk/lifelonglearninginquiry/docs/IFLL-Sector-Paper1.pdf.

Coates, J. & Leahy, T. (2006) Ideology and politics: essential factors in the path towards sustainability. *Electronic Green Journal*, 23.

Cohen, R. & Kennedy, P. (2012) *Global Sociology*, 3rd ed. Basingstoke: Palgrave Macmillan.

Craft, A. (2000) *Continuing Professional Development: A Practical Guide for Teachers and Schools*, 2nd ed. London: Routledge-Falmer.

Curtis, W. & Pettigrew, A. (2010) *Education Studies: Reflective Reader*. Exeter: Learning Matters.

Czerniawski, G. (2011) *Engaging Teachers and Globalisation*. Abingdon: Routledge.

Dawe, G., Jucker, R. & Martin, S. (2005) *Sustainable Development in Higher Education: Current Practice and Future Developments: A Report for The Higher Education Academy*. Available at www.heacademy.ac.uk/misc/executivesummary.pdf.

Dewey, J. (1933/1989) *Essays and How We Think*, Rev. ed. Carbondale: Southern University Press.

DfE (2011) *Schools, Pupils and their Characteristics: January 2011*. London: DfE.

DfES (2001) *Schools Achieving Success*. Annesley: DfES Publications.

DfES (2004) *Every Child Matters: Change for Children*. London: Department for Education and Skills.

Doherty, J. & Jarvis, P. (2016) Continuing professional development, in P. Jarvis et al. (eds.), *The Complete Companion for Teaching and Leading Practice in the Early Years*. Abingdon: Routledge.

Edwards, C. (1997) *Changing Places? Flexibility, Lifelong Learning and a Learning Society*. London: Routledge.

Edwards, R. & Usher, R. (2000) *Globalisation and Pedagogy: Space, Place and Identity*. London: Routledge.

Elliott, A. (2002) Beck's sociology of risk: a critical assessment. *Sociology*, 36(2), 293-315.

Emirbayer, M. & Mische, A. (1998) What is agency? *The American Journal of Sociology*, 103(4), 962-1023.

Freire, P. (1993) *Pedagogy of the Oppressed*. London: Penguin Books.

Gaultner, A. & Green, R. (2015) Promoting the inclusion of migrant children in a UK school. *Educational and Child Psychology*, 32(4), 39-51.

Giddens, A. (1991) *Modernity and Self-Identity: Society in the Late Modern Age*. Stamford: Stamford University Press.

Goodson, I.F. (1989) Sponsoring the teacher's voice. *Cambridge Journal of Education*, 21(1), 35-45.

Goodson, I.F. (2000) The principled professional, *Prospects*, 30(2).

Goodson, I.F. & Rudd, T. (2016) The limits of neoliberal education: refraction, reinterpretation and reimagination, in T. Rudd and I.F. Goodson (eds.), *Negotiating Neo Liberalism: Developing Alternative Educational Visions*. London: Sense Publishers.

Habermas, J. (1972) *Knowledge and Human Interests*. London: Heinemann.

Hargreaves, A. (2000) Professionals and parents: a social movement for educational change, in N. Bascia & A. Hargreaves (eds.), *The Sharp Edge of Educational Change: Teaching, Leading and the Realities of Reform*. London: Routledge Falmer.

Hargreaves, A. (2003) *Teaching in the Knowledge Society*. Maidenhead: Open University Press

Hargreaves, A. & Lo, L.N.K. (2000) The paradoxical profession: teaching at the turn of the century. *Prospects*, 30(2), 167-180.

Harvey, D. (1990) *The Condition Of Postmodernity: An Enquiry into the Origins of Cultural Change*. Cambridge, MA: Blackwell.

Held, D., McGrew, A., Goldblatt, D. & Perraton. J. (1999) *Global Transformations: Politics, Economics and Culture*. Stanford: Stanford University Press.

Helterbran, V.R. (2005) Lifelong learning: a stratagem for new teachers. *Academic Exchange Quarterly*, 9(4), 250-254.

Hicks, D. (2004) Radical education, in S. Ward (ed.), *Education Studies: A Student's Guide*. Abingdon: Routledge.

Hill, B.V. (2014) The schooling of ethics. *Educational Philosophy and Theory*, 46(3), 296-310.

Ife, J. (2008) *Human Rights and Social Work*. New York: Cambridge University Press.

Karlberg, M. (2008) Discourse, identity, and global citizenship. *Peace Review: A Journal of Social Justice*, 20, 310-320.

Keating, A., Kerr, D., Benton, T., Mundy, E. & Lopes, J. (2010) *Citizenship Education in England 2001-2010: Young People's Practices and Prospects for the Future: The Eighth and Final Report from the Citizenship Education Longitudinal Study (CELS)*. London: DfE.

Keddie, A. (2014) Political justice, schooling and issues of group identity. *Educational Philosophy and Theory*, 46(1), 100-111.

Kemmis, S. (1993) Action research, in M. Hammersley (ed.), *Educational Research: Current Issues*. London: Paul Chapman Publishing

Kemmis, S., Cole, P. & Suggett, D. (1983) *Towards a Socially Critical School: Orientations to Curriculum and Transition*. Melbourne: Victorian Institute of Secondary Education.

Kuit, J.A., Reay, J. & Freeman, R. (2001) Experiences of reflective teaching. *Active Learning in Higher Education*, 2(2), 128-142.

Lechner, F. (2009) *Globalization: The Making of World Society*. London: Wiley.

Mackay, H. (2000) The globalization of culture, in D. Held (ed.), *A Globalizing World? Culture, Economics and Politics*. London: Routledge.

Meadows, D. (2001) Dancing with systems. *Whole Earth, Winter*. Available at www.wholeearthmag.com/ArticleBin/447.html.

Mezirow, J. (2000) *Learning as Transformation: Critical Perspectives on a Theory in Progress*. San Francisco: Jossey-Bass Publishers.

Modood, T. (2010) *Still Not Easy Being British: Struggles for a Multicultural Citizenship*. Stoke on Trent: Trentham Books.

Newman, L. & Dale, A. (2005) The role of agency in sustainable local community development. *Local Environment*, 10(5), 477-486.

Noddings, N. (2010) Moral education in an age of globalization. *Educational Philosophy and Theory Special Issue: Local Pedagogies/Global Ethics*, 42(4), 390-396.

Peters, S. & Wals, A.E.J. (2013) Learning and knowing in pursuit of sustainability: concepts and tools for trans-disciplinary environmental research, in M. Krasny & J. Dillon (eds.), *Trading Zones In Environmental Education: Creating Trans-Disciplinary Dialogue*. New York: Peter Lang.

Pike, G. & Selby, D. (1999) *In the Global Classroom 1*. Toronto: Pippin.

Pike, G. & Selby, D. (2000) *In the Global Classroom 2*. Toronto: Pippin.

Reynolds, M. (2001) Education for inclusion, teacher education and the teacher training agency standards. *Journal of In-Service Training*, 27(3), 465-476.

Reynolds, R. & Vinterek, M. (2013) Globalization and classroom practice: insights on learning about the world in Swedish and Australian schools. *Nordidactica: Journal of Humanities and Social Science Education*, 2013(1), 104-130.

Ritzer, G. (2010) *Globalization: A Basic Text*. Chichester: Wiley.

Robertson, R. (1992) *Globalization: Social Theory and Global Culture*. London: Sage Publications.

Robinson, C. (2014) *Children, their Voices and their Experience of School: What Does the Evidence Tell Us?* York: Cambridge Primary Review Trust.

Schirato, T. & Webb, J. (2003) *Understanding Globalization*. London: Sage.

Schön, D. (1998) *Educating the Reflective Practitioner: Toward a New Design for Teaching and Learning in Professions*. Oxford: Jossey Bass.

Schweisfurth, M. (2013) Learner-centred education in international perspective. *Journal of International and Comparative Education*, 2(1), 1-8.

Scott, W. (2002) *Sustainability and Learning: What Role for the Curriculum*. University of Bath: University of Bath, CREE.

Selby, D. (1999) Global education: towards and quantum model of environmental education. *Canadian Journal of Environmental Education*, 4, 125-141.

Selby, D. (2005) Responding to globalisation and the global condition. Technocratic skills or normative ideals? A critique of Douglas Bourne's conception of global education. *Zeitschrift fur Bildungsforschung und*

Entwicklungspadagogik (Journal for International Education Research and Development Education), 28(1), 35-39.

Sellars, M. (2017) *Reflective Practice for Teachers*, 2nd ed. London: Sage.

Sen, A. (2007) Capability and well-being, in D.M. Hausman (ed.), *The Philosophy of Economics: An Anthology*, 3rd ed. Cambridge: Cambridge University Press.

Sen, A. (2013) The ends and means of sustainability. *Journal of Human Development and Capabilities: A Multi-Disciplinary Journal for People-Centered Development*, 14(1), 6-20. Available at www.tandfonline.com/doi/pdf/10.1080/19452829.2012.747492.

Sterling, S. (2004) An analysis of the development of sustainability education internationally: evolution, interpretation and transformative potential, in J. Blewitt and C. Cullingford (eds.), *The Sustainability Curriculum: The Challenge for Higher Education*. London: Earthscan.

Sterling, S. (2011) Transformative learning and sustainability: sketching the conceptual ground. *Learning and Teaching in Higher Education*, 5, 17-33.

Tomlinson, J. (2003) Globalization and cultural identity, in A.J. McGrew & J. Held (eds.), *The Global Transformations Reader: An Introduction to the Globalization Debate*, 2nd ed. Cambridge: Polity Press.

Torabian, E. (2014) WTO/GATS and the global governance of education: a holistic analysis of its impacts on teachers' professionalism. *Educate*, 14(3), 44-59.

Turner, M.K. (2005) Sustainability: principles and practice, in M. Redclift (ed.), *Sustainability: Critical Concepts in the Social Sciences*. Abingdon: Routledge.

UNESCO (2005) Values of Sustainable Development. Available at www.unesco.org/new/en/education/themes/leading-the-international-agenda/education-for-sustainable-development/sustainable-development/values-sd/.

United Nations Human Rights (1989). Convention on the Rights of the Child. Available at www.ohchr.org/en/professionalinterest/pages/crc.aspx.

Urry, J. (2000) Mobile sociology. *The British Journal of Sociology*, 51, 185-203.

Vandeyar, S. (2017) The teacher as an agent of meaningful educational change. *Educational Sciences: Theory and Practice*, 17, 373-393.

Vidovich, L. (2006) *'Travelling' Policy: Contesting 'Global' Policy Trends in Educational Accountability*. TASA Conference. Available from https://tasa.org.au/wp-content/uploads/2015/02/Vidovich.pdf.

Vulliamy, G. (2010) *Educational Reform in a Globalised Age: What is Globalisation and How is it Affecting Education World-Wide?* Available at www.ncyu.edu.tw/files/site_content/geche/1-Educational%20Reform%20in%20a%20Globalised%20Age%20What%20is%20globalisation%20and%20how%20is%20it%20affecting%20education%20world-wide1.pdf.

Walker, M. (2012) A capital or capabilities education narrative in a world of staggering inequalities? *International Journal of Educational Development*, 32(3), 384-393.

Wals, A.E.J. (2012) *Shaping the Education of Tomorrow*. Hamburg: UNESCO.

Wals, A.E.J. & Jickling, B. (2002). 'Sustainability' in higher education: from doublethink and newspeak to critical thinking and meaningful learning, *Higher Education Policy*, 15, 121–131.

World Commission on Environment and Development (WCED) (1987) *Our Common Future*. Oxford: Oxford University Press.

Yang, Y. & Valdés-Cotera, R. (2011) *Conceptual Evolution and Policy Developments in Lifelong Learning*. Hamburg: UNESCO Institute for Lifelong Learning.

Young, M.F.D. (1998) *The Curriculum of the Future: From the New Sociology of Education to a Critical Theory of Learning*. London: Falmer Press.

5 Hidden childhoods

The unseen challenges facing professionals in schools today

Sean MacBlain

Introduction

Significant numbers of teachers in the UK and especially England are leaving the profession after only a few years feeling unhappy and demotivated due largely to what many describe as extremely high and unnecessary workloads (MacBlain & Purdy, 2011; Menzies et al., 2015). A predominating view found among many teachers is one of seeing their professional integrity continually compromised, due mainly to ever-shifting political landscapes and imposed ideologies that have little real substance in theories of learning. The extent to which political influence pervades education is well documented; less than a decade ago, Smidt (2011, p. 85), for example, referenced the celebrated theorist and educationalist Jerome Bruner, as follows: 'Bruner said that we should treat education for what it is, and for him what it was was political.' This chapter examines key challenges facing teachers in the UK today that are, arguably, failing to be recognised and resourced by successive governments.

> **By the end of the chapter you will:**
>
> - Have explored significant and largely unrecognised challenges that impact upon the professional practice of teachers today.
> - Have examined contradictions between the growing recognition that childhood and children's learning today is highly complex, and recent government-led ideologies and initiatives.
> - Have explored how childhood educators can position themselves within policy and practice while maintaining their personal values and beliefs on how to meet the individual needs of each child in their care.

Agreed or imposed ideologies: the challenges

Hidden beneath the veneer of imposed requirements of teachers by successive governments lie challenging and concerning elements of

21st-century childhood that have not yet been adequately appraised, nor properly understood (MacBlain, Dunn & Luke, 2017). Arguably, childhood in the UK has become overly characterised and in some instances defined by issues around safeguarding, social breakdown, increased materialism and over-sexualisation, excessive reliance on digitalisation and social networking and a breakdown of family structures, all of which lead to an absence of consistency and stability in the lives of many children. Within this context teachers are tasked with publicly demonstrating how they meet target-driven standards with their professional practice being continually monitored and scrutinised.

Teachers are now, more than ever before, held accountable for meeting the requirements of an educational system that has been largely prescribed by policy and decision-makers (Adams, Monahan & Wills, 2015; Lea, 2013; MacBlain, 2014; Moss, 2015). They must increasingly interpret how the ever-shifting and politically imposed drivers that have come to dominate the ethos of most schools affect their professional practice (Pillen, Beijaard & den Brok, 2013; Troman, 2008). More particularly, they also need to understand how they, as agents of these drivers, willingly or unwillingly collaborate with imposed systems and processes by successive governments that all-too-frequently fail to meet the holistic needs of significant numbers of children. Those aspiring to become teachers are now confronted with having to critically examine their own understanding of current and imposed political agendas and how they might develop strategies that enable them to sustain accepted professional practice while holding on to personal ideals and beliefs in the moral and social purposes of education (Ryan & Bourke, 2013). They must also critically engage in thinking about how they might develop their own resilience and maintain any personal beliefs that might conflict with government-led ideologies and imposed requirements that challenge their integrity and even militate against any visions they might have of educating children holistically.

Pause to reflect

Take time to view the following You Tube video, 'Teachers leaving the profession to teach abroad' by Francis Gilbert: www.youtube.com/watch?v=uj2jm9zGkYw (published on 4 March 2016) and consider what needs to be happen in the UK to keep teachers in the profession.

The impact of poverty

Many teachers today find themselves working with children who are growing up in homes characterised by high levels of poverty with little access to suitable reading materials and digital technology, poor nutrition and sparse sleeping arrangements. Professional standards now require teachers to understand the impact of poverty on children's learning as well as on their social and emotional development; they are expected to adjust their practice and compensate in ways that minimise the impact of poverty on those children in their care (MacBlain, 2014; MacBlain et al., 2017; Wilshaw, 2014). This is, by any standard, an ambitious expectation and, in practice, can result in teachers having to draw heavily on their own emotional reserves and resilience. They must be seen to demonstrate objectivity that is underpinned by strong empathy, understanding and what the theorist and philosopher Nel Noddings has referred to, as 'relational caring' (Noddings, 2005). Some teachers may struggle with these more personal aspects of children's learning and may find themselves experiencing high levels of stress, coupled with anxieties that emerge from their own feelings of being unable to effect material as well as emotional change in the lives of their pupils (MacBlain and Purdy, 2011).

Poverty impacts upon schools in a multitude of obscure and unseen ways and its effects are not always apparent and may, all-too-frequently, go unrecognised. The effects of poverty are typically disguised by children who fear embarrassment, teasing from their peers, name-calling and even bullying. To be taunted by others for 'failing' to have the 'right' clothes or the up-to-date digital accessories can, for many children, be the stuff of nightmares, leaving their teachers with the often unnecessary and disquieting burden of facing up to quite major inequalities among their pupils and, once again, drawing upon their own emotional reserves. The effect of poverty on children and the challenges it can present to the professional practice of many teachers should not be viewed as being of a trivial nature.

Less than a decade ago, Cullis and Hansen (2009), in commenting on lower-income families in the UK emphasised how every £100 of extra income in the first nine months of a child's life made the difference of around one month of development by the age of five. They further emphasised how the poorest families in society are frequently unable to afford books and computers, not to mention extracurricular activities. They also drew attention to how children's education is more likely to be adversely affected by poor nutrition, overcrowding in the home, and by anxiety and stress. Field (2010, p. 28) also drew public attention to how children growing up in low-income families in the UK frequently grow up to become 'poor adults' and are more likely to present with conduct disorders and behavioural issues even in their preschool years. They are also, Field asserted, more likely to encounter bullying, do less well at school and engage during adolescence in unnecessary and potentially dangerous risk-taking behaviours.

In a report entitled *Deprivation and Risk: The Case for Early Intervention* (Action for Children, 2010), Dr Ruth Lupton commented on the striking relationship between deprivation and educational attainment in children coming from the poorest homes. Lupton drew special attention to how children from such homes began school with more limited vocabularies than their counterparts and were more likely to present with conduct disorders and hyperactive behaviour patterns. Even more worryingly, she drew attention to an issue facing many teachers in primary schools in the UK who must now account for standards in literacy and numeracy when inspected and when their schools are cited in league tables, 'even the brightest children from the most disadvantaged backgrounds are overtaken by the age of 10 by their better-off peers who start off behind them' (p.12).

A further and concerning feature of poverty that challenges the professionalism of many teachers is the growing recognition that children from the poorest families who are intellectually very able, frequently fail to find their way into schools that are high-achieving and academically inspiring (MacBlain etal., 2017; Sharma, 2007); this is a factor that teachers can do little about but that impacts heavily upon their capacity to achieve government-imposed targets. In his annual report, *Unsure Start: HMCI's Early Years Annual Report 2012/13*, Sir Michael Wilshaw, Her Majesty's Chief Inspector (Ofsted) emphasised in the starkest of ways how poverty and low-income – especially in the early years – can impact significantly on children's future realisations of potential and ultimately their life choices. He emphasised how very young children from the poorest backgrounds, 'are less likely to follow instructions, make themselves understood, manage their own basic hygiene or play well together'. Sir Michael went on to stress how by the time they started formal education at age four, most children will have started to read simple words, will be talking in sentences and will be able to perform simple numerical operations. This was in contrast, he asserted to, how far fewer children from the poorest families in the UK, 'can do these things well'. Children from low-income families, he stressed, are much more likely to 'lag behind at age three' than their better-off peers, 'Too many do badly by the end of primary, and carry on doing badly at the end of secondary' (Wilshaw, 2014, p. 3). Sir Michael then went on to emphasise the financial cost to the nation, which at a time of growing austerity and increased economic competition among countries across the globe is, again, very concerning:

> If the gap isn't closed, the costs to our nation will run into billions. The Sutton Trust estimates that the UK's economy would see cumulative losses of up to £1.3 trillion in GDP [gross domestic product] over the next 40 years if the country fails to bring the educational outcomes of children from poorer homes up to the UK average.
>
> (Wilshaw, 2014, p. 3)

In addressing concerns regarding the underachievement of children in England, Sir Michael called for changes in the way that many children from low-income families needed to be taught. Such a view, although welcomed, does to some extent question the professionalism of teachers working in schools where there are high percentages of children from low-income households.

It has been recognised for some time (Sharma, 2007) that by six years of age, children who are intellectually less able and who grow up in rich families are likely to have overtaken intellectually able children growing up in poor families. Here again, we see factors beyond the control of teachers but which they are held accountable for. Less than a decade ago, in one part of the UK, Northern Ireland, a report entitled, *The Way Forward for Special Educational Needs and Inclusion* (DENI, 2009, p. 12), which provided an analysis of underachievement in schools stressed how 'poor educational attainment can reinforce the cycle of deprivation that many... marginalised groups experience throughout their lives'. A subsequent UK government report, *A New Approach to Child Poverty: Tackling the Causes of Disadvantage and Transforming Families* (GOV.UK, 2011), revealed how some 800,000 children in families with a disabled member were living in relative poverty. The report also concluded that children from black and ethnic families were twice as likely to live in poverty as those from white families and that more than a million children in lone-parent families were also living in relative poverty. These numbers have increased in past years with greater recognition now being given to the impact of recent austerity and downturn in the global economy. A further group of children whose needs have only recently come to be recognised are those children, of all ages, who find themselves having to care for a parent or an older sibling.

Caring for others: the challenge of broken childhoods

In addition to dealing with the growing impact of austerity and poverty, teachers may find themselves having to manage the emotional needs of children who from an early age, find themselves having to care for parents or older siblings.

Case study

Ben is five years of age and lives with his mother who was diagnosed some years ago with acute arthritis and shortly afterwards with a brain tumour. Each morning Ben helps to get his mother out of bed and makes her breakfast before leaving for school. When he returns from school he spends time preparing the evening meal and on alternate

> days help to wash his mother. Ms Jones, Ben's teacher – who has only recently qualified – is very aware of Ben's home life and takes time every day to sit with him and talk through any difficulties she feels Ben is experiencing. She finds that Ben gets very upset when he talks about home and his mother and is quick to become tearful. While Ms Jones works closely with the head teacher regarding Ben's situation and on occasions has met with the family's social worker, she finds the nature of Ben's problems to be very upsetting and at times finds herself tearful and experiencing problems with sleeping. She herself lost her father when very young following a long period of illness and Ben's difficulties and emotional state bring back difficult memories for her. She feels at times that she must put on a brave face in front of Ben to maintain her professional standing but feels depressed by the lack of support Ben and his mother are receiving from agencies outside of the school. She feels particularly upset on Friday afternoons as she knows what Ben is going home to.

The number of children in the UK who are caring for others is consider-able (MacBlain, 2014; MacBlain et al., 2017); the impact of this on children's learning and development has only recently begun to be recognised and prop-erly understood (MacBlain et al., 2017). Here again, teachers are expected, as in the case of Ben's teacher above, to demonstrate critical and informed understanding of the deeper emotional and social impact that caring for an older member of the family can have on their pupils' learning. This can be particularly challenging for newly qualified teachers, particularly when they are faced with scrutiny by inspection bodies.

In 2015, the Barnardo's organisation reported that the average age of a young carer in the UK was 12, defining young carers as those children and young people below the age of 18 who, 'provide regular and on-going care and emotional support to a family member who is physically or men-tally ill, disabled or misuses substances'. Barnardo's cited the 2001 census, which had identified 175,000 young carers in the UK, of which some 13,000 were caring for someone for more than 50 hours per week. Barnardo's also indicated how in 2011, the census had identified 178,000 young carers in England and Wales, indicating a significant increase of 83 per cent in the number of young carers aged between the ages of five and seven and a 55 per cent increase between the ages of eight and nine years. Such numbers suggest that many teachers will be working daily with children who are not only caring for someone else but, importantly, are having to look after them-selves at home. The impact upon these children's education and develop-ment will be substantial.

The challenges of social and emotional deprivation

Arguably, the professionalism of teachers is being more publicly tested today than ever before by increasing levels of socially created problems, the likes of which have not been witnessed since Victorian time.

Case study

Jonathan has just begun his first teaching post as a Key Stage 1 teacher in an inner-city primary school where there are high levels of social deprivation. He has been informed by the head teacher that a high number of children in his class come from homes where their parents are known to be Class A drug users with heavy involvement from social services. He becomes quickly aware that many of the children in his class are presenting with conduct disorders and behavioural issues as well as emotional issues. He has been told by his head teacher that he must focus on the teaching of phonics and record the individual progress of each child in this area, as the school was recently downgraded following an inspection. Jonathan feels that he should be giving more focus to managing behavioural issues than focusing on teaching phonics, which he is aware will support the children in accessing literacy. He neverthe-less struggles with what he feels is an imposition from the head teacher who is anxious about any follow-up inspections. He wonders if he has made the right decision to become a teacher.

In a review undertaken by the National Society for the Prevention of Cruelty to Children (NSPCC; Cuthbert et al., 2011) it was estimated that in 2010, 19,500 infants under the age of one year in the UK were living in a home with a parent who was a user of Class A drugs and 93,500 infants were living in a home with a parent who was a problem drinker. In 2012 alone, the NSPCC found itself dealing with 30,000 cases or 0.25 per cent of the population. It has also been recognised (Walker, Flatley & Kershaw, 2009) that domestic violence accounts for around 14 per cent of all violent incidents in England and Wales and that 6 per cent of children receive maltreatment at the hands of their parents or carers, with 7 per cent of children experiencing serious physical abuse (Cawson, 2002). An estimated 6 per cent of children have been subjects of serious absence of care throughout their childhood, with the same percentage of children experiencing frequent and severe emotional maltreatment.

It has been reported (CYPMHC, 2012) that in an average classroom, ten children will have witnessed the separation of their parents and one child will have experienced the death of a parent. In 2014, 40,000 children in the UK experienced the death of a parent (NCB, 2016). A year later, the Barnardo's organisation reported the average age of young carers in the UK as 12 years, citing the 2001 census, which identified 175,000 young carers, of which 13,000 were caring for someone for more than 50 hours per week. Barnardo's also indicated how in the ten years following the census, there were 178,000 young carers in England and Wales representing an increase of 83 per cent of young carers aged between five and seven years of age and of 55 per cent aged between eight and nine years.

Issues of class: increased choice or veiled elitism

Only five years ago, the notion of 'class' and segregation in UK schools was brought forcibly to the public's attention when Kershaw (2012), writing in the UK *i-Newspaper*, *The Independent*, drew public attention in her article to comments made by Dr Mary Bousted, then general secretary of the Association of Teachers and Lecturers (ATL) as follows:

> Dr Mary Bousted... said stratified schools are 'toxic' for deprived youngsters... 'We have schools for the elite; schools for the middle class and schools for the working class. Too few schools have mixed intakes... The effect of unbalanced school intakes is toxic for the poorest and most dispossessed...'

The article went on to indicate how Bousted had stressed that while teachers and school leaders had been straining 'every sinew to raise aspiration and achievement, they struggle always against the effects of poverty, ill health and deprivation' emphasising how, 'children in these schools routinely fail to make the educational progress achieved by their more advantaged peers'. In the article, Bousted was reported as referring to how government had cut funding to Sure Start centres, how they had scrapped the education maintenance allowance for teenagers from poorer homes, taken away protected funding for school meals and had introduced tax reforms that, she suggested, 'are likely to hit low to middle-income families'. It is, of course, important to recognise that the above comments were offered by an individual who was representing union members, although perhaps not every single member of that union. Here, it is possible to locate different ideologies that are underpinning perceptions of learning and the communities into which children arrive for their formal education as well as those communities from where they come.

Multiculturalism: opportunities and challenges

The cultural make-up of most schools in the UK and, thereby, the educational experiences of many children has changed dramatically in previous decades as many 'new arrivals' enter the education system across the UK (MacBlain and Purdy, 2011; MacBlain et al., 2017). This is mirrored in other

European countries and across the globe with the situation in the UK and across Europe being more recently exacerbated by large numbers of children, young people and families escaping conflict in the Middle East. Prior to the Coalition government in the UK coming to power in 2010, it was recorded that there were 856,670 pupils learning English as an Additional Language (EAL) in England representing 15.2 per cent of the primary school population and 11.1 per cent of the secondary school population in England. with it being estimated that there were more than 200 languages being spoken (DCSF, 2009). In inner London, it was further reported at the time that 54.1 per cent of pupils were learning English as an additional language (DCSF 2009). The National Association for Language Development in the Curriculum (NALDIC, 2012) reported on their website how the results of the annual School Census in January of that year had shown that:

> one in six primary school pupils in England – 577,555 – do not have English as their first language. In secondary schools the figure stands at 417,765, just over one in eight. Once special schools and pupil referral units are taken into account, the total rises to just over a million at 1,007,090. These figures have doubled since 1997.

Across the UK, the picture has been similar with, for example, Northern Ireland seeing a dramatic increase in new arrivals over the past few decades. Statistics from the Department of Education Northern Ireland (DENI, 2010) indicated a sixfold increase in what was termed 'newcomer children' between 2001/2002 (1,366 children) and 2009/2010 (7,899 children) across schools in Northern Ireland, with more than 50 per cent of these children being educated in primary schools in 2009–2010 (DENI, 2010). Such developments have had implications for teachers. One challenge facing many teachers has been the increased numbers of children entering schools with little if any English. In 2012, the National Association for Language Development in the Curriculum (NALDIC) again reported, as follows:

> There are more than a million children between 5-16 years old in UK schools who speak in excess of 360 languages between them in addition to English. Currently there are 1,061,010 bilingual 5-16 year olds in English schools, 26,131 in Scotland, 8674 'newcomer' pupils in Northern Ireland and 30,756 EAL learners in Wales.

While such an increase brings with it many benefits, it also presents many challenges for teachers and the demands placed upon them. Once again, it can be argued that while teachers strive to maintain standards of professionalism and to do the best for their pupils, the world around them is changing and the levels of support they feel they need to maintain standards are decreasing. This would appear to be particularly so with newly qualified teachers (NQTs) who, although being trained to high standards, must quickly adapt to the challenges they face as full-time practitioners with high levels of accountability and responsibility for meeting government-imposed targets and ensuring that their school will always be able to deal with changing inspection frameworks.

The continuing challenges of inclusion

The increase in diversity that has occurred across the UK in recent decades is directly associated with not only more children with special educational needs (SEN) and/or disability being educated in mainstream schools following a landmark international towards greater inclusion (UNICEF 1989; UNESCO 1994) but importantly a number of legislative landmarks such as the 1981 Education Act (which was subsequently repealed) and the Special Education Needs Disability Act (SENDA 2001), which have aimed at strengthening the rights of these groups of children. More recently, in September 2014, the Children and Families Act came into effect in England, followed in January 2015 by a new Code of Practice. This Act, and the subsequent Code of Practice have significantly change the nature of special educational needs and/or disability education. For example, the Act encompasses health with education and social services and places legal obligations on local authorities and professionals to view interventions with children and young people as now being from 0 to 25 years of age. Importantly, the Act places children at the centre of decision-making and involves families much more in any processes affecting their children.

Legislation has been accompanied by a growing shift in attitudes towards children with additional needs over the past few decades and the importance of educating these children in mainstream settings. In England, for example, it has been estimated that in 2008 there were 1,614,300 children with SEN in mainstream schools or around 20 per cent of the school population (DCSF, 2008). Statistics for other parts of the UK have yielded similar figures with, for example, Northern Ireland demonstrating that in 2009 there were around 60,000 children with SEN in mainstream schools, amounting to some 18 per cent of the whole school population. The number of children with additional needs in mainstream schools across the UK is now considerable and regarded as the norm. While inclusion of children with SEN within mainstream settings has been generally applauded, it has brought with it significant challenges for teachers as they have strived to meet the needs of an increasingly diverse and culturally different school population.

New childhoods in a digital age

Teachers are often heard to complain that technology is dominating the lives of too many children and that too few children engage in active, collaborative and physical play. They view this as directly affecting the learning of many of their pupils who spend considerable amounts of time each week on digital media. The impact of this can even be seen in the quality of children's play. Much of children's play is radically different to that of previous years. Just under a decade ago, McDowall highlighted what is a worrying trend and one that impacts indirectly on those aspects of the wider curriculum, such as creativity, self-realisation and emotional and social development, that teachers strive to create in their classrooms:

> Children do not play out in the street anymore, they are rarely allowed to travel to school on their own... Children spend an increasing proportion of their time in specially designated places such as day nurseries, out-of-school clubs and their own bedrooms, frequently fitted out with the latest technology. Childhood is progressively more regulated so that instead of being a natural part of public life, it takes place in private.
>
> (McDowall Clark, 2010, p.1)

Increasingly, children's play is becoming characterised by a reliance on technology (Beauchamp, 2006, 2012), which although not necessarily a bad thing, can, however, become problematic if it dominates play and, thereby, reduces other types of play activities. The growing concerns at the heart of the debate around play and its impact on children's learning was brought to the public's attention in February 2012 when Graeme Paton, education editor for the national online UK newspaper *The Telegraph*, reported as follows:

> In a letter to *The Daily Telegraph*, academics and authors said that controversial education reforms are robbing under-fives of the ability to play and leading to the 'schoolification' of the early years... today's letter... warned of 'widespread concern about the direction of the current revision'... The experts... suggested the system was 'too inflexible to cater for the highly diverse developmental needs of young children'. They are now creating a new group... to push for an alternative curriculum.

It is recognised and accepted by most practitioners (MacBlain et al., 2017) that, through play, children learn to cooperate with others, manage relationships and come to understand the world they live in. It is through play that children develop abilities and skills with language and in doing so, progress their capacity to think (Gray & MacBlain, 2015). The exaggerated accountability that is now placed on teachers means, in practice, that they are often wary to encourage younger children to engage in play activities as a means of learning.

Quality: reality or illusion

While the *quality* of children's learning experiences is rightly seen as crucially important to their education and especially the case in early childhood education, this is a word that is often bandied about but rarely defined with any real clarity (Apple, 2013; Campbell-Barr & Leeson, 2016; Moss, 2014). It can be argued with a high degree of certainty that within the UK and especially England there has been over the past decades a multitude of government-led initiatives combined with exceptional levels of political interference and regulation, leading to an educational landscape that is especially challenging for young children and their teachers in addition to early years practitioners (Heimer & Klefstad, 2015; MacBlain et al., 2017). This challenge rightly includes maintaining a professional stance in the face of increased political interference and discourse that can stifle critical debates around what professionalism needs to look like (Osgood, 2010, p. 119). Worryingly, Campbell-Barr and Leeson (2016) suggest that underpinning the existing systems that dominate government ideologies are a collective set of assumptions about childhood that are offered as certainties but are rarely, if ever, questioned. From the perspective of government, there appears to be no real appetite for debating such certainties; this can, in part, be evidenced by the fact that little, if any recognition of alternative perspectives appears to be given by policy and decision-makers (Moss & Dahlberg, 2008).

An apparent contradiction to many is that while we acquire much greater understanding of the complex nature of children's learning (Gray & MacBlain, 2015) there appears, at the same time, to be a strong desire on the part of successive UK governments to coerce teachers into accepting overly simplified and questionable 'algorithms of accountability'; this, in addition to overly formalised and prescriptive standards in practice (MacBlain et al., 2017). As Moss (2015) suggests, the greater the complexity, the greater the desire among policy- and decision-makers to implement systems and processes that have reduction and control at their heart. For example, while the thorny problem of how to determine and account for teacher effectiveness continues to exercise the thinking of academics and remains hugely inconsistent, policymakers have gone ahead and developed over the past three decades questionable methods for measuring the effectiveness of teaching through inspection frameworks (Range, Duncan, Day Scherz & Haines, 2012). It appears to be the case that many policy- and decision-makers have embraced quantitative methods as a means of evaluating quality and the effectiveness of teachers. These methods also appear to have been embraced as a means of identifying patterns and trends that can then be used to highlight and emphasise comparisons between schools, which have, in England, formed the basis for what are reliably suspect league tables and data dashboards that Lea (2013, p. 23) has referred to as blunt instruments used to 'rank organisational compliance with policy objectives... devised to assist consumers, not citizens, to choose their "preferred" educational service'.

Chapter summary

When policy becomes established, the ideologies underpinning it largely define professional identity and what is then generally accepted as good practice in the education of children. Teachers are then required to practise within an artificially constructed context, which largely defines what 'quality' should look like. While some form of artificial individualism appears to remain, the reality is that it does so only through a prescriptive framework that is defined and regulated through data-driven performance and accountability. Debate, then, becomes restricted and superficial and, perhaps most worryingly, threatening to those values promoted by some policy- and decision-makers. Hidden beneath many of the imposed conditions and requirements by recent governments and ever-increasing scrutiny by inspection bodies are new and concerning elements in childhood that have not been properly recognised and are poorly understood but that society expects teachers to manage in what are largely government-prescribed ways that they may have little if any faith in.

References

Action for Children (2010) *Deprivation and Risk: The Case for Early Intervention*. London: Action for Children.

Adams, K., Monahan, J. & Wills, R. (2015) Losing the whole child? A national survey of primary education training provision for spiritual, moral, social and cultural development. *European Journal of Teacher Education*, 38(2), 119-216.

Apple, M.W. (2013) *Can Education Change Society?* Abingdon: Routledge.

Barnardo's (2015) *Child Poverty Statistics and Facts*. Available at www.barnardos.org.uk/what_we_do/our_work/child_poverty/child_poverty_what_is_poverty/child_poverty_statistics_facts.htm.

Beauchamp, G. (2006) New technologies and 'new teaching': a process of evolution? in R. Webb (ed.), *Changing Teaching and Learning in the Primary School*. Maidenhead: Open University Press.

Beauchamp, G. (2012) *ICT in the Primary School: From Pedagogy to Practice*. London: Pearson.

Campbell-Barr, V. & Leeson, C. (2016) *Quality & Leadership in the Early Years: Research, Theory & Practice*. London: Sage.

Cawson, P. (2002) *Child Maltreatment in the Family*. London: NSPCC.

Cullis, A. & Hansen, K. (2009) *Child Development in the First Three Sweeps of the Millennium Cohort Study*. DCSF Research Report RW-007.

Cuthbert, C., Rayns, G. and Stanley, K. (2011) *All Babies Count, Prevention and Protection for Vulnerable Babies: A Review of the Evidence*. London: NSPCC.

CYPMHC (2012) *Resilience and Results: How to Improve the Emotional and Mental Wellbeing of Children and Young People in Your School*. The Children and Young People's Mental Health Coalition.

Department for Children, Schools and Families (DCSF) (2008) *Special Educational Needs in England*. London: DCSF.

Department for Children, Schools and Families (DCSF) (2009) Statistical First Release August 2009. London: DCSF.

Department of Education Northern Ireland (DENI) (2009) *The Way Forward for Special Educational Needs and Inclusion*. Bangor: DENI.

Department of Education Northern Ireland (DENI) (2010) *Statistics on Education*. Bangor: DENI. Available at www.deni.gov.uk.

Field, F. (2010) *The Foundation Years: Preventing Poor Children Becoming Poor Adults, Report of the Independent Review on Poverty and Life Chances*. London: Cabinet Office.

GOV.UK (2011) *A New Approach to Child Poverty: Tackling the Causes of Disadvantage and Transforming Families*. Norwich: The Stationery Office.

Gray, C. & MacBlain, S.F. (2015) *Learning Theories in Childhood*, 2nd ed. London: Sage.

Heimer, L.G. & Klefstad, E. (2015) 'It's not really a menu because we can't pick what we do': context integration in kindergarten contexts. *Global Studies in Childhood*, 5(3), 239–254.

Kershaw, A. (2012) School intake 'segregated by class'. *i-Newspaper, The Independent*, 4 April. Available at www.independent.co.uk/news/education/education-news/school-intake-segregated-by-class-7618824.html.

Lea, S. (2013) Early years work, professionalism and the translation of policy into practice, in Z. Kingdon & J. Gourd (eds.), *Early Years Policy: The Impact on Practice*. London: Routledge.

MacBlain, S.F. (2014) *How Children Learn*. London: Sage.

MacBlain, S.F., Dunn, J. & Luke, I. (2017) *Contemporary Childhood: New Perspectives*. London: Sage.

MacBlain, S.F. & Purdy, N. (2011) Confidence or confusion: how prepared are today's NQTs to meet the additional needs of children in schools? *Journal of Teacher Development*, 3(15), 381–394.

McDowall Clark, R. (2010) *Childhood in Society: for Early Childhood Studies*. Exeter: Learning Matters Ltd.

Menzies, L., Parameshwaran, M., Trethewey, A., Shaw, B., Baars, S. & Chiong, C. (2015) *Why Teach?* LKMco and Person report. Available at http://whyteach.lkmco.org.

Moss, P. (2014) *Transformative Change and Real Utopias in Early Childhood Education: A Story of Democracy, Experimentation and Potentiality*. Abingdon: Brighton.

Moss, P. (2015) There are alternatives! Contestation and hope in early childhood education. *Global Studies of Childhood*, 5(3), 226-238.

Moss, P. & Dahlberg, G. (2008) Beyond quality in early childhood education and care – languages of evaluation. *New Zealand Journal of Teachers' Work*, 5(1), 3-12.

National Association for Language Development in the Curriculum (NALDIC) (2012) Available at www.naldic.org.uk/research-and-information/eal-statistics/eal-pupils.

National Children's Bureau (NCB) (2016) *Children's Grief Awareness Week – 40,000 Children Bereaved of a Parent Each Year*. Available at www.ncb.org.uk/news/childrens-grief-awareness-week-40000-children-bereaved-of-a-parent-each-year.

Noddings, N. (2005) Caring in education, in *The Encyclopedia of Informal Education*. Available at www.infed.org/biblio/noddings_caring_in_education.htm.

Osgood, J. (2010) Reconstructing professionalism in ECEC: the case for the critically reflective emotional professional. *Early Years: An International Research Journal*, 30(2), 119-133.

Paton, G. (2012) New-style 'nappy curriculum' will damage childhood. *Daily Telegraph*, 6 February. Available at www.telegraph.co.uk/education/educationnews/9064870/New-style-nappy-curriculum-will-damage-childhood.html.

Pillen, M., Beijaard, D. & den Brok, P. (2013) Tensions in beginning teachers' professional identity development, accompanying feelings and coping strategies. *European Journal of Teacher Education*, 36(3), 240-260.

Range, B.G., Duncan, H.E., Day Scherz, S. & Haines, C.A. (2012) School leaders' perceptions about incompetent teachers: implications for supervision and evaluation. *NASSP Bulletin*, 96(4), 302-322.

Ryan, M. & Bourke, T. (2013) The teacher as reflexive professional: making visible the excluded discourse in teacher standards, *Discourse: Studies in the Cultural Politics of Education*, 34(3), 411-423.

Sharma, N. (2007) *'It Doesn't Happen Here': The Reality of Child Poverty in the UK*. Ilford: Barnardo Press.

Smidt, S. (2011) *Introducing Bruner: A Guide for Practitioners and Students in Early Years Education*. London: Routledge.

Troman, G. (2008) Primary teacher identity, commitment and career in performative school cultures. *British Educational Research Journal*, 34(5), 619-633.

United Nations Children's Fund (UNICEF) (1989) *Convention on the Rights of the Child*. Available at www2.ohchr.org/english/law/crc.htm#art12.

United Nations Educational, Scientific and Cultural Organization (UNESCO) (1994) *The Salamanca Statement and Framework For Action On Special Needs Education*. Accessed at http://unesdoc.unesco.org/images/0009/000984/098427eo.pdf.

Walker, A., Flatley, J. & Kershaw, C. (eds.) (2009) *Crime in England and Wales 2008/09.* Vol. 1, *Findings from the British Crime Survey and Police Recorded Crime.* London: HMSO.

Wilshaw, M. (2014) *Unsure Start: HMCI's Early Years Annual Report 2012/13.* Speech 2014.

6 Creativity and purpose in the curriculum

Gill Golder

Introduction

It is very evident that education has purpose; by definition, it would suggest that it is primarily concerned with the promotion of learning. The purpose of education appears to be different according to where in the world you are in education, in what educational system you are educated and on the design of the curriculum you experience to become educated. Claxton and Lucas (2013, p. 8) suggest that, 'there is no such thing as "best practice" in teaching, or a "world-class" school... until you say what the desired outcomes are. Best practice – for what? World class – at what?'

Education and learning are complex. Research over the past few decades has made statements around the purpose of education and what it is to be educated. Bailey (1984) suggested that it is its capacity to liberate a person from the here and now by involving pupils in what is fundamental and general and intrinsically worthwhile in order to promote the development of the capacity to think that characterises education. Peters (1966) suggested that an educated person is not merely competent at performing a particular task, rather their competence is linked to a much wider belief system. Peters' comments around a wider belief system are echoed in Menter's (2014) suggestion that a wider consideration of what is considered pedagogy by teachers can be learned together with the need to find a personal ethos for practice, technical skills and basic classroom practices. This notion that a teacher's beliefs and values influence how they teach and to a certain extent what they teach is supported by Shulman (2005) who suggests that signature pedagogies involve *choice*; a selection of alternative approaches that assist active learners.

By the end of the chapter you will:

- Have an understanding of the difference between creative teaching and the concept of learning creatively.
- Have considered theoretical models of creative teaching and learning.

Creativity in the educational context

Bano, Naseer and Zainab (2014, p. 598) suggested that there are four components associated with creativity, notably, 'a creative person has fluency in generating ideas, there is flexibility, a creative person possess originality in his/her ideas, and he/she have an elaboration of ideas'.

Edwards (2001, p. 222) states that creativity engages, 'the openness to ideas and the willingness to encourage the exploration of the unknown, even if not easily manageable'. However, the problems with investigating creativity in schools comes from the multiple definitions of it. 'Despite the abundance of definitions of creativity and related terms, few are widely used and many researchers simply avoid defining relevant terms at all' (Plucker & Makel, 2010, p. 48).

In England, the status and perceived importance of creativity in schools has ebbed and flowed. At the turn of the century, creativity appeared on the ascendancy with the NACCCE (1999) report, which promoted democratic creativity. It highlighted the importance of developing creative capacities through 'a balance of teaching skills and understanding, and promoting the freedom to innovate and take risks' (p. 10). In this way, creative achievements were attainable in all fields of life and for all individuals. This acted as catalyst for a series of initiatives and policy developments including *creative development* and *personal learning and thinking skills* (PLTS) embedded in the 2007 Foundation Stage and in 2008 National Curriculum respectively. There was the emergence of the Qualification, Curriculum Authority's (QCA) focus on creativity in schools in 2005 and by 2006 the Roberts Review and the government response (DfES, 2006) had mapped out a cross-phase framework for creativity from early years to the initial training and professional development of teachers. By 2008 the McMaster report (DCMS, 2008) laid a new emphasis on *cultural learning* rather than *creative learning*, launching ten regional pilots called the 'Cultural Offer'. By 2010 the new Coalition government brought out its White Paper (DfE, 2010), in which there was no clarity on how creativity was to be supported or conceptualised in school, the slimmed-down National Curriculum followed in 2012 that removed PLTS and only briefly touched upon creativity. By 2012 a new report was commissioned, the Henley report (DCMS, 2012), that emphasised the role of 'cultural education' targeting creative industries; the subsequent Cultural Education document (DCMS & DfE, 2013) highlighted how the curriculum and qualification reforms intended to secure high-quality teaching and qualifications in arts subjects and that, 'all young people should experience excellent teaching which helps them develop their cultural knowledge, understanding and skills' (p. 8). What is evident from this look at the *history* of policy is that the term *cultural education* has replaced *creative education*, but also appears to reinforce the notion that both creativity and cultural development are the proviso of the Arts, far from NACCCE's (1999) view of democratic creativity accessible to all, in all fields of life.

Nevertheless, it may be that schools now have greater flexibility in how they approach creativity. What may emerge from the apparent waning of the visibility of creative education in policy is that schools are now freer to explore creative pedagogies on their own terms rather than having creativity subjected to legislative frameworks (Craft, Cremin, Clack & Hay, 2013).

Pause to reflect

Consider the following aspects for the context in which you work:

- How does the organisational climate of my school serve to stimulate creativity?
- What else could your educational institution do to foster creativity?
- How are teachers encouraged to be creative in my teaching?

The tension between accountability and creativity

Standards and accountability have become a central issue of educational reform in many countries (Møller, 2009). In the current *self-improving system* evident in UK schools, Gilbert (2012) argues that there are two key approaches to accountability. The first and most embedded is a performance or productivity model that is summative and designed to prove quality. It emphasises outputs such as test and exam results (Elliott, Bridges, Ebbutt, Gibson & Nias, 1981). The second is an improvement or process model that emphasises school evaluation, opening practice to critique and debate. Hopkins (2007) suggests that this model is more formative as it is designed to improve quality. Despite increased autonomy for schools, in particular in the UK, the balance of accountability activities is strongly focused on the current public accountability framework and it is argued that the process model needs to assume greater importance as it offers more leverage for change (Gilbert, 2012). Bailey (2010) suggests that in schools only certain kinds of learning are *privileged*; for example, the learning of examination specification content or National Curriculum coverage. There are, however, an infinite amount of things that could be learnt and we need to ask how the curriculum has been selected. The increase in high stakes accountability and the tensions arising from this has resulted in what Sahlberg (2011) describes as barriers to creativity in schools. Sahlberg (2014) continues to suggest that the emphasis on high-stakes testing and standardisation reduces the potential for deep learning. Nadelson et al. (2012) echo *concerns of tension* in their study, suggesting that opportunities for creative expression, teacher professional autonomy and classroom effectiveness would be negatively perceived by teachers because of the influence of standards-based reform.

Raising the profile of creativity

Despite the powerful emphasis on higher achievement in a narrower set of core subjects and the ways in which schools are held accountable for these, Craft (2011) suggests that there are three drivers that are raising the profile of creativity in education, these being the *economic driver*, the *social driver* and the *technological driver*.

The economic driver has arisen from the requirements to develop a work-force who are innovators and are able to respond flexibility to the changes in demands of economic development. In the neoliberal era where the free market, entrepreneurial initiative, private enterprise, consumer choice and government de-regulation are central in business practice (Ross & Gibson, 2006), Craft (2011) suggests that successful businesses have creative practices as a key feature to their success. Florida (2002) suggests that creativity is held as one of the most important competencies by 21st-century employers, but also identifies that employability and competitiveness are the reasons that creativity is acknowledged by and promoted through policy.

Craft (2011) describes the social driver as a factor that has arisen from changes in, 'social and emotional mobility' and the associated move away from obligation to choice; this is also a feature of neoliberalism with a move from the notion of 'the public good' or 'community' and replacing it with 'individual responsibility' (Martinez & Garcia, 2000).

The technological driver both offers and demands opportunities for creativity, to meet the pace of change and development in digital technologies. The UK Commission for Employment and Skills (2012, p. 23) released a report that highlighted the inextricable link between the 'digital and creative sector' identifying the performance challenges, the 'real-life' skills solutions and the need to create 'rapidly changing sets of skills needed to work with new technologies and deliver creative content at a technical and professional level'.

Notably, Craft and Hall (2015, p. 19) suggest that there are some 'fundamental tensions and dilemmas inherent in developing creativity' that go beyond tension between policy and practice or accountability. The first is that of culture and creativity and the opportunities afforded to teachers to make the most of the how creativity can manifest itself in the classroom from diverse cultural contexts. Craft and Hall suggest that this is currently under-explored or scrutinised in teachers' practice. The second is creativity in the environment; our creative side often stems from the environment we surround ourselves with. Craft and Hall (2015) suggest that the environment in which children learn is heavily influenced by increased globalisation and marketisation. The third is ethics and using creativity or creative practices to balance conflicting perspectives and values, which Craft and Hall (2015) imply may be irreconcilable. Finally, there is the balance between the development of creativity and knowledge in schools and how pedagogical solutions may be found to confront the tensions and dilemmas.

Pause to reflect

- How should the current accountability system evolve to support a more autonomous and self-improving system?
- What can teachers do to balance the tensions between accountability and creativity?

Signature pedagogies

One vehicle to unpick the tensions and dilemmas in addressing creativity in teaching and learning is to explore *signature pedagogies*. Research exploring how different disciplines instigated the idea of signature pedagogies was conducted with doctoral students (Golde, 2007; Guring, Chick & Haynie, 2009; Shulman, 2005). A consensus developed from this research which suggests that disciplines have both common pedagogical approaches but also distinctive practices.

Shulman (2005, p. 59) argues that signature pedagogies, 'form habits of head, heart and hand'. According to Shulman, there are three dimensions to signature pedagogies.

> First, it has a surface structure which consists of the concrete operational acts of teaching and learning [...] Any signature pedagogy also has a deep structure. A set of assumptions about how is best to impart a certain body of knowledge and know-how. And it has an implicit structure, a moral dimension that comprises of a set of beliefs about professional attitude, values and dispositions.
>
> (Shulman, 2005, pp. 54-55)

Interestingly, Sullivan, Colby, Wegner, Bond and Shulman (2007) add a fourth component of signature pedagogy, illustrated in Figure 6.1, when considering legal professions, but this could equality apply to education and the teaching profession.

Creative pedagogy

The notion of creative pedagogy as a distinct form of pedagogy was introduced by Aleinikov (1989) and is made up of a number of distinctive

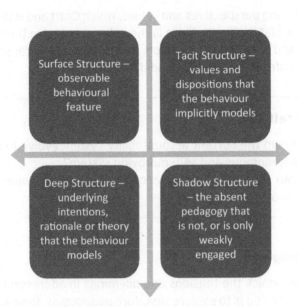

Figure 6.1 Shuman's signature pedagogy composition

components that help learners to learn creatively, transform classrooms into creative and flexible learning environments, allow learners to innovate and create and enable risk-taking and thinking imaginatively.

Lin (2011) describes creative pedagogy from three different perspectives: creative teaching, teaching for creativity and creative learning. In this model, creative learning focuses on children's action and embraces children's intrinsic curiosity in tuition; creative teaching as innovative and imaginative approach to teaching, the actions of the teacher including improvisational elements in tuition; and the final element of Lin's creative pedagogies is a creativity-supporting environment that facilitates physical and social contexts in an open-minded atmosphere that supports and inspires learning. Teaching for creativity aims for creative learning and the development of a creative person (Craft, 2005, pp. 41-42).

Teaching creatively and developing pupils' creativity

The NACCCE (1999, p. 29) defined creativity as 'Imaginative Pause to reflect fashioned so as to produce outcomes that are original and of value'. Lucas and Greany (2000) suggest that teaching creatively is underpinned by pedagogies that draw upon pupil perspectives, and involve high levels of pupil participation and collaboration. However, creativity should not just be seen as a pedagogy or a teacher's responsibility to teach creatively; rather it should also be explored from the learner's perspective as well as creating environments where creativity can thrive. This is supported by Jeffrey and Craft (2004), who suggest that teachers should both teach creatively and teach *for* creativity; teaching creativity should involve some spontaneity and creative teaching is more likely to result in creativity in pupil response.

Signature creative pedagogies

Thompson and Hall (2014) suggest that signature creative pedagogies intertwine knowledge and action with the way we are in the world, the nature of existence. Thompson and Hall (2014) continue to note that creative practitioners value collaborative and cooperative ways of working so have axiological commitment. From these perspectives it is possible to develop an analytical framework which proposes three components; *pedagogy, pedagogic platforms*, and *purposes and practices*. Thompson and Hall's (2014) report combines these three components to generate a creative signature pedagogy (see Figure 6.2 for an overview of these components).

Learning disposition, learning power and creativity

Focusing on a signature pedagogy for creativity provides a useful understanding of how the patterns of actions, activities and interactions by a teacher for a specific class can generate conditions for creative teaching and learning to take place. As Facer (2011) and Moss and Petrie (2002) suggest, the concept of pedagogy encompasses relations, learning environments, rules, culture, conversations and norms within a wider social context. However, missing from this model of creative pedagogies is an understanding of what creative pedagogy might look like from a learner's perspective and knowing whether by considering platform, purposes and practices there is a generation of effective outcomes regarding creative skills or dispositions.

Buckingham Shum and Crick (2012) suggest that there is growing evidence that an examination of learning dispositions (i.e., a learner's orientation towards learning) provides useful information regarding the nature of learners' engagement with new learning opportunities in both formal and informal contexts. Buckingham Shum and Crick (2012, p. 1) also note that while an obvious critical yardstick in learning is *mastery of discipline knowledge* as defined by an explicit curriculum, in order to understand mastery learning you need to understand, 'learning dispositions and the transferable competencies associated with skilful learning' in different contexts.

Alongside learning dispositions, Crick, Broadfoot and Claxton (2004) argue that there is a need to examine learning power. They identify seven dimensions needed to harness what is hypothesised to be 'the power to learn', measured through the Effective Lifelong Learning Inventory (ELLI). The dimensions they state are *change and learning, critical curiosity,*

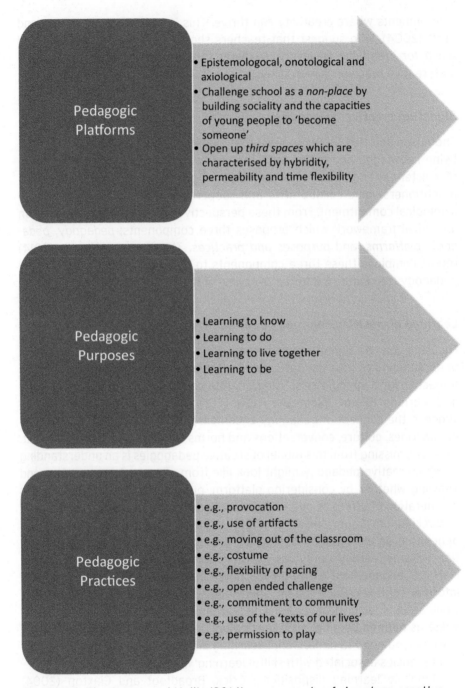

Pedagogic Platforms

- Epistemologocal, onotological and axiological
- Challenge school as a *non-place* by building sociality and the capacities of young people to 'become someone'
- Open up *third spaces* which are characterised by hybridity, permeability and time flexibility

Pedagogic Purposes

- Learning to know
- Learning to do
- Learning to live together
- Learning to be

Pedagogic Practices

- e.g., provocation
- e.g., use of artifacts
- e.g., moving out of the classroom
- e.g., costume
- e.g., flexibility of pacing
- e.g., open ended challenge
- e.g., commitment to community
- e.g., use of the 'texts of our lives'
- e.g., permission to play

Figure 6.2 Thompson and Hall's (2014) components of signature creative pedagogies

meaning-making, dependence and fragility, creativity, learning relationships and *strategic awareness.* By completing the inventory, an individual learner profile can be generated to enable learners, teachers and mentors to reflect on learning.

It is valuable to consider how disposition and learning power models have utilised the notion of creativity and the implications of a creative approach. Two models are offered for examination.

The five creative dispositions model

This model provides a means of providing a theoretical underpinning for defining and assessing creativity. The model explores what creativity is, and the potential benefits of creativity being developed and tracked in schools. They drew on a myriad of research into creatively that explored differing views of creativity, the value of assessing creativity, individual versus social competencies of creativity, subject specific versus generic creativity, and learnable versus innate creativity. From this they developed the *five disposition model* (Figure 6.3) with 15 subdivisions and three elements of tracking to assess the development of a creative aspect. These latter three elements are:

> Strength – this was seen in the level of independence demonstrated by pupils in terms of their need for teacher prompts or scaffolding, or their need for favourable conditions;
>
> Breadth – this was seen in the tendency of pupils to exercise creative dispositions in new contexts, or in a new domain; and
>
> Depth – this was seen in the level of sophistication of disposition application and the extent to which application of dispositions was appropriate to the occasion.
>
> (Lucas, Claxton & Spencer, 2013, p.18)

The transformative education model: 4Cs learning approach

In this model, 4Cs (creativity, critical reflection, communication and collaboration) are capabilities that through the lens of critical pedagogy explore ways in which all schools can transform teaching and learning. Jefferson and Anderson (2017) suggest that the interaction of knowledge, new understanding and wisdom can develop through the 4Cs to develop deep understanding, connect knowledge and promote transformative learning.

A common feature of both models is the notion of organising knowledge development for a deeper learning; they both suggest learning strategies that might be akin to generative learning theory. According to Fiorella and Mayer (2015), generative learning theory is where learning is a sense-making

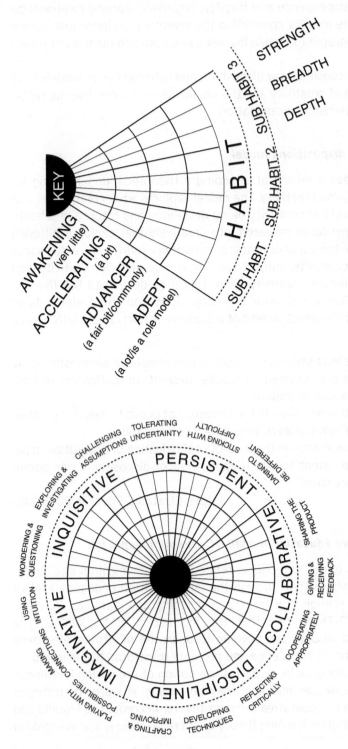

Figure 6.3 Fifteen subdivisions for creativity (Lucas, Claxton and Spencer, 2013, p.18)

process that involves building cognitive structures that can be used in new situations. It is argued that further research into signature pedagogies and research on generative learning strategies would benefit from a greater focus on assessing meaningful learning outcomes such as the dispositions by Lucas et al. (2013) and the capabilities identified by Jefferson and Anderson (2017), rather than rote learning outcomes such as recall.

Pause to reflect

- Consider how three components of pedagogy, pedagogic platforms, purposes and practices manifest themselves in your own developing practice.
- Consider where your practice already embeds developing learners' capabilities or dispositions, and how current assessment practices take account for these.

Chapter summary

This chapter has explored creativity in the educational context, the tension between accountability and creativity and the research supporting teaching creatively and developing pupils' creativity. It considered how teachers are balancing the drive for high academic attainment with the benefits for the learner and society on developing creativity, exploring different curriculum models that engender both. In exploring models that highlight creativity and dispositions to learning, the challenge for teachers is to enable and empower learners to develop depth of knowledge by creating a learning environment and adopting a pedagogy that fosters self-regulated learners. In this creative context, both the teacher and the pupil are able to develop agency and a sense of control over their own learning. This sense of control allows a feeling of wellbeing that helps both the teacher and the learner to flourish and thrive (Seligman, Ernst, Gillham, Reivich & Linkins, 2009).

We need innovative practitioner research within the field of curriculum and assessment studies – research that will change assessment policy and creative learning practices within the classroom in different socio-cultural contexts.

(Lucas et al., 2013, pp. 140–149)

References

Aleinikov, A.G. (1989) On creative pedagogy. *Higher Education Bulletin*, 12, 29–34.

Bailey, C. (1984) *Beyond the Present and Particular: A Theory of Liberal Education*. London: Routledge & Kegan Paul.

Bailey, R. (2010) *The Philosophy of Education: An Introduction*. London: Continuum.

Bano, A., Naseer, N. & Zainab, D. (2014) Creativity and academic performance of primary school children. *Pakistan Journal of Social Sciences*, 34(2), 597–606.

Buckingham Shum, S. & Crick, R. (2012) Learning dispositions and transferable competencies: pedagogy, modelling and learning analytics. *Proceeding of the 2nd International Conference on Learning Analytics & Knowledge*, 29 April–2 May, Vancouver, BC. New York: ACM Press.

Claxton, G. & Lucas, B. (2013) *Redesigning Schooling: What Kind of Teaching for What Kind of Learning?* London: SSAT.

Craft, A. (2005) *Creativity in Schools: Tensions and Dilemmas*. London: Routledge.

Craft, A. (2011) *Creativity and Education Futures: Learning in a Digital Age*. Stoke on Trent: Trentham Books Ltd.

Craft, A., Cremin, T., Clack, J. & Hay, P. (2013) Creative primary schools developing and maintaining pedagogy for creativity. *Ethnography for Education*, 9(1), 16–34.

Craft A. & Hall E. (2015) Change in the landscape for creativity in education, in A. Wilson (ed.), *Creativity in Primary Education*. London: Sage.

Crick, R., Broadfoot, P. & Claxton, G. (2004) Developing an effective life-long learning inventory: the ELLI project. *Assessment in Education*, 11(3), 248–272.

DCMS (2008) *Supporting Excellence in the Arts: From Measurement to Judgement*. London: DCMS.

DCMS (2012) *Cultural Education in England*. London: DCMS.

DCMS & DfE (2013) *Cultural Education: A Summary of Programmes and Opportunities*. London: DCMS.

Delors, J. (1996) *Learning: The Treasure Within*. Paris: UNESCO.

DfE (2010) *The Importance of Teaching: The Schools White Paper*. London: DfE.

DfES (2006) *Government Response to Paul Roberts' Report on Nurturing Creativity in Young People*. London: DfES.

Edwards, S.M. (2001) The technology paradox: efficiency versus creativity. *Creativity Research Journal*, 12(13), 221–228.

Elliott, J., Bridges, D., Ebbutt, D., Gibson, R. & Nias, J. (1981) *School Accountability: The SSRC Cambridge Accountability Project*. London: Grant McIntyre Limited.

Facer, K. (2011) *Learning Futures: Education, Technology and Socio-Technical Change*. London: Routledge.

Fiorella, L. & Mayer, R.E. (2015) *Learning as a Generative Pause to Reflect: Eight Learning Strategies that Promote Understanding*. New York: Cambridge University Press.

Florida, R. (2002) *The Rise of the Creative Class... and How it's Transforming Work, Leisure, Community and Everyday Life*. New York: Basic Books

Gilbert, C. (2012) *Towards a Self-Improving System: The Role of School Accountability*. Nottingham: NCLS.

Golde, C. (2007) Signature pedagogies in doctoral education: are they adaptable to the preparation of education researchers? *Educational Researcher*, 36(6), 344-351.

Goodson, I. (2000) The principled professional, *Prospects*, 30(2), 182-188.

Guring, R.A.R., Chick, N. & Haynie, A. (eds.) (2009) *Exploring Signature Pedagogies: Approaches to Teaching Disciplinary Habits of Mind*. Sterling: Stylus.

Hopkins, D. (2007) *Every School a Great School*. Buckinghamshire: Open University Press, McGraw-Hill.

Jefferson, M. & Anderson, M. (2017) *Transforming Schools' Creativity, Critical Reflection, Communication, Collaboration*. London: Bloomsbury.

Jeffrey, B. & Craft, A. (2004) Teaching creatively and teaching for creativity: distinctions and relationships. *Educational Studies*, 30(1), 77-87.

Lin, Y.-S. (2011) Fostering creativity through education – a conceptual framework of creative pedagogy. *Creative Education*, 2(3), 149-155.

Lucas, B., Claxton, G. & Spencer, E. (2013) Progression in student creativity in school: first steps towards new forms of formative assessments. *OECD Education Working Papers*, No. 86. Paris: OECD Publishing. Available at http://dx.doi.org/10.1787/5k4dp59msdwk-en.

Lucas, B. & Greany, T. (2000) *Learning to Learn: Setting the Agenda for Schools in the 21st Century*. London: Campaign for Learning.

Martinez, E. & Garcia, A. (2000) What is 'neo-liberalism'? A brief definition, in E.W. Ross & R. Gibson (eds.), *Neoliberalism and Education Reform*. New Jersey: Hampton Press.

Menter, I. (2014) *Developing Creative and Critical Educational Practitioners*. Northwich: Victoria Door Critical Publishing.

Møller, J. (2009) School leadership in an age of accountability: tensions between managerial and professional accountability. *Journal of Educational Change*, 10(1), 37-46.

Moss, P. & Petrie, P. (2002) *From Children's Services to Children's Spaces: Public Policy, Children and Childhood*. London: Routledge Falmer.

Nadelson, L., Fuller, M., Briggs, P., Hammons, D., Bubak, K. & Sass, M. (2012) The tension between teacher accountability and flexibility: the paradox of standards-based reform. *Teacher Education and Practice*, 25(2), 196-220.

National Advisory Committee on Creative and Cultural Education (NACCCE) (1999) *All Our Futures: Creativity, Culture and Education*. London: DCMS and DfEE.

Peters, R.S. (1966) *Ethics and Education*. London: Allen and Unwin.

Plucker, J. & Makel, M. (2010) Assessment of creativity, in J. Kaufman & R. Sternberg (eds.), *The Cambridge Handbook of Creativity*. Cambridge: Cambridge University Press.

QCA (2005) *Creativity, Find it! Promote it! Promoting Pupils Creative Thinking and Behaviour across the Curriculum Key Stage 1, 2 & 3 - Practical Materials for Schools*. London: QCA.

Ross, E.W. & Gibson, R. (2006) *Neoliberalism and Education Reform*. Creskill, New Jersey: Hampton Press.

Sahlberg, P. (2011) The role of education in promoting creativity: potential barriers and enabling factors, in R. Schenkel & O. Quintin (eds.), *Measuring Creativity*. Brussels: European Commission.

Sahlberg, P. (2014) *Finish Lessons 2.0: What Can the World Learn from Educational Change in Finland?* Willeston: Teacher's College Press.

Seligman, M.E.P., Ernst, R.M., Gillham, J., Reivich, K. & Linkins, M. (2009) Positive education: positive psychology and classroom interventions. *Oxford Review of Education*, 3(35), 293-311.

Shulman, L.S. (2005) Signature pedagogies in the professions. *Daedalus*, 134(3), 52-59.

Sullivan, W., Colby, A., Wegner, J., Bond, L. & Shulman, L. (2007) *Educating Lawyers: Preparation for the Profession of Law*. San Francisco: Jossey-Bass.

Thomson, P. & Hall, C. (2014) The signature pedagogies of creative practitioners, in K. Westphal, U. Stadler-Altmann, S. Schittler, and W. Lohfield (eds.), *Raume Kultureller Bildung Beltz Juventa*. Weinhein Basel: Beltz Juventa.

Thomson, P., Hall, C., Jones, K. & Sefton Green, J. (2012) *The Signature Pedagogies Project: Final Report*. Newcastle upon Tyne: Creativity, Culture and Education.

UK Commission for Employment and Skills (2012) *Sector Skills Insights: Digital and Creative*. Rotherham: UKCES.

PART III

Laying the foundations for the thriving professional

7 Resilience and wellbeing in childhood
Education and therapy
Hazel Bending

Introduction

In this chapter we are looking at wellbeing and resilience, and what schools and education colleagues can to do support positive wellbeing and the development of resilience in the school community, and, therefore, to enable professionals to thrive.

By the end of the chapter you will:

- Understand the concepts of wellbeing and resilience.
- Be able to identify the factors that support and challenge wellbeing.
- Develop an understanding of how education practice can challenge and support wellbeing.

Wellbeing

Wellbeing is a multifaceted construct which indicates an individual's sense of happiness, satisfaction and meaning in life. How we view wellbeing can, to an extent, depend on our philosophical approach. Do you err towards Bentham, Locke and Hobbes? If so then you are more likely to equate wellbeing with subjectiveness, pleasure and happiness (Diener, 2009), while followers of Aristotle are more likely to equate wellbeing with meaningful life, virtue and seeking potential (Norton, 1976). Increasingly common is the view that wellbeing is less of a dichotomy between these two facets, and more likely to be an integrated construct, in which an individual makes subjective evaluations of not only their affective experiences but also of their overall satisfaction in life and current role/position in addition to their sense of autonomy, control, competence, connectedness and congruence.

> **Pause to reflect**
>
> Think about your own wellbeing. How do you rate your sense of autonomy, control, competence and connectedness with peers/colleagues?

Factors that impact on wellbeing

A number of chronic factors impact on overall wellbeing in children. Mathieson, Tambs and Dalgard (1999) argue that chronic (long-lasting) stressors damage wellbeing far more than sudden extreme events. Chronic stressors for children include; low social economic status and poverty (Lupien, King, Meaney & McEwen, 2001; Fell & Hewstone, 2015), which reduces the opportunities of social integration and cohesion with peers. Environmental factors, such as violence in the home, neglect and sexual abuse (UNICEF, n.d.; Jutte et al., 2015; Collin-Vezina, Daigneault & Herbert, 2013), which often results in the child withdrawing from friendships and becoming increasingly isolated. For those children who are taken into care, the NSPCC (2014) found that they were four times more likely to have mental health problems and poor wellbeing in contrast to their peers. Research has identified that children with intellectual disabilities and those with hearing loss have been found to have lower levels of life satisfaction than their peers (Brantley, Huebner & Nagle, 2002; Gilman, Easterbrooks & Frey, 2004).

It is not just the home environment that impacts on a child's sense of wellbeing. Children spend 25 per cent of their day in school. This environment plays a major role in a child's sense of wellbeing. A child in school with little autonomy and control over their choice of peers or friendships is likely to have a lower sense of wellbeing than a child who feels connected to their school, part of a community that has strong boundaries, clear expectations and the opportunity to influence the environment. Further to this, a child who is happy and has a positive sense of wellbeing is more likely to work towards reaching their academic goals, they are more actively engaged in activities that interest them (Diener, Lucas & Oishi, 2002), and they achieve academically (Suldo & Shaffer, 2008). In contrast, lower wellbeing impacts on self-worth, concentration, attendance and behaviour in the classroom (Mani, Mullainathan, Shafir & Zhao, 2013). Consequently, a number of governmental policies are driving the increase of the provision of *therapy in the classroom*.

Of particular note is *Future in Mind* (Department of Health & NHS England, 2015), which sets out the new Children and Young People's Mental Health and Wellbeing Taskforce's plan of promoting good mental wellbeing and resilience, preventing mental health problems and early identification of need in young people and children, within the broader context of our society. This was followed by *Mental Health and Behaviour in Schools* (Department of Education, 2016), which outlined the Department's view on the association of behaviour in classrooms and unidentified mental health problems, setting out the role of schools in relation to supporting children to develop resilience, wellbeing and positive mental health. This policy differentiates between the role of the school in enabling those in need to access additional and alternative services, and the 'in house' provision provided by teaching and other staff within the school premises. It further identifies a number of strategies teachers could employ, many which are reflected in the list at the end of this chapter, in order to promote wellbeing and resilience among the children in their care.

Therapy in the classroom

When considering the notion of *therapy in the classroom*, it is not about providing input outside of the curriculum, as this might take you outside of your professional boundaries, but about providing opportunities within the curriculum and other classroom practices that will enable children to develop a sense of autonomy, control, competence, connectedness and congruence. For example, enabling children to decide which sport to play in a PE lesson, focusing on strengths and abilities to increase the sense of competence, to providing relationships and an atmosphere that encourages children to talk among themselves and with adults about their goals, achievements and problems. As the personal factors that underpin resilience are learnt, transferrable and adaptable, what a child learns in one arena can be utilised in another.

Roffey (2012) states that it is important to focus on strengths rather than problems. By focusing on strengths we are encouraging individuals to make positive evaluations about their sense of wellbeing, and this increases their likelihood of utilising coping skills and other protective factors in a multitude of situations. This supports not only a sense of wellbeing, but also resilience, which we will discuss in the next section. Further to this the Department of Education (2016) recommend that input offered in schools to support and develop children's wellbeing should be provided to the whole cohort, and not just targeted at those who are in need. By doing so, this serves to build a *healthy school*, encourages cohesion, helps children (and staff) identify and develop protective factors, which are fundamental to resiliency, and enables schools to make early identification of potential problems.

It is now understood that the teacher has a fundamental role in providing an atmosphere and safe environment in which solutions, ideas and problems can be aired by choice by all members of the school community. In schools, like all institutions, it is the relationships between people that impact on their sense of wellbeing, therefore, it is equally important to consider the wellbeing of the teacher, as well as the children. A low sense of wellbeing in teachers impacts on their performance, access to knowledge, ability to offer and build warm and encouraging relationships with the children and colleagues and increases both absenteeism and presenteeism (Kidger et al., 2016; Jennings & Greenberg, 2009), which in turn impact on the quantity and quality of the education environment. Furthermore, at present, up to a third of teachers leave the profession within their first five years of teaching (Savage, 2017), while not all leave due to negative wellbeing, a sense of autonomy, control, competence, connectedness and congruence all assist in supporting longevity within a profession.

Section summary

Developing a sense of autonomy, control, competence and connectedness within our classrooms and schools can help develop child and adult wellbeing.

Pause to reflect

- What factors do you think impact on a teacher's sense of wellbeing?
- Focusing on strengths, what factors do you think support a teacher's sense of wellbeing?

In this section we have looked broadly at wellbeing and the factors that influence this subjective sense of happiness, satisfaction and meaning in life. By answering the questions in the reflection boxes, you have been able to assess your own wellbeing. Now would be a good point to think about how you can develop a positive sense of wellbeing, by reducing your contact with the negative influences and move to a position in which you can manage the impact of chronic stressors to improve your overall sense of wellbeing.

The final part of this section looked at the wellbeing of a teacher, the factors that influence negative wellbeing and those that support positive wellbeing. If you have not done so, now is the time to identify your support systems, who supports your wellbeing? The identification of these individuals is the starting place to identifying your protective factors that support your resilience in the classroom and life.

Resilience

In this section we will address the socially constructed concept of resilience; what is it and protective factors.

Pause to reflect

Before we begin
Can you think of a time when you faced a challenge, hazard or stressor? How did you react? What did you do? What/who supported you through it?

Resilience is a dynamic process, in which an individual positively adapts and responds to risk, adversity and challenge. While some overcome such hazards, others falter (Rutter, 1987). Resilience is a positive function that enables individuals to utilise coping strategies, it is not inherent, nor is it a fixed trait, it is not mental health, wellbeing or social competence. It is learnt via interaction. Rutter (2006) argues that resilience is an acquired trait, that we develop resilience through interaction with the social environment. There is wide variation between individuals interacting with the same stressor. It is dependent on time and place, therefore there is wide variation between individuals and from the same individual at different times with similar and different stressors. Finally, resilience is dependent on protective factors, these factors are elements that exist within an individual's social environment that support the use of coping skills, encourage autonomy, offer choice and control and provide the individual with a sense of community or connectedness to others.

Lazarus and Folkman (1984) suggest that coping skills are cognitive and that behavioural efforts are performed to manage specific stressors that have been appraised as being taxing or exceeding the person's resources. Coping enables the individual to either regulate the stressful situation (emotional-focused coping) or amend the person-environment relationship that is causing the stress (problem-focused coping).

Life events can provide opportunities for an individual to utilise their coping skills and develop resilience. Such life events can be divided into two categories; normative and non-normative. Normative transitions are those that are expected due to the society, age or culture of the individual, such as changes in the frontal lobes in adolescence enabling the development of executive functions, the transition from primary to secondary school or the deployment of a parent in the armed forces. Non-normative transitions are unexpected, and to the individual unique, such as divorce, parental death and crime. While it is said 'what doesn't kill you makes you stronger', transition through these life events, both expected or otherwise, requires a complex interrelation between an individual's protective factors, with some increasing in order to minimise the risk to the individual's wellbeing and enhance the opportunity for a good outcome.

> **Pause to reflect**
>
> Before we move onto protective factors, go back to your original list of stressors, challenges and life hazards and add in the normative transitions that you have faced. How did you react? What did you do? What supported you through the events?

Protective factors

How an individual deals with a stressor or decides which coping mechanism to use depends on the protective factors available in their social environment. Research has demonstrated that there are three categories of protective factors; individual characteristics, family relations and supportive environments (Mellor, 2007).

Individual characteristics

Rutter (1987) identified that a number of individual differences, such as gender, cognitive skills and temperament have a moderating influence on the individual's use of resiliency. A number of authors (Mellor, 2007) have identified how gender influences peer relationships and construction of friend and friendships in children, close friendships based around secrets and sharing tend to lead to more supportive friendships in times of stressors. These offer the young person a range of peers that they can turn to for support, confidence and problem-solving.

Executive functions of the brain are the core cognitive functions that enable us to select, maintain and attain goals, solve problems, attend to information and be flexible. The neurological basis of the executive functions is within the frontal lobes, consequently maturation is not reached until after synaptic pruning and myelination in adolescence (see Siegel, 2014). Younger children utilise basic cognitive skills such as inhibition and emotional regulation when dealing with a stressor, but are generally unable to solve complex problems independently. As maturation is on an individual timetable, and developed through interaction with the environments, it means that some young people are able to utilise these executive functions earlier, while others reach this point long after schooling has ended.

Finally, temperament, functionality of two key areas within the human brain - the limbic system, which supports bottom-up processing of information and emotional response, and the orbito-frontal cortex, which supports top-down processing and self-regulation in stressful situations - and the balance between these two areas impacts on how an individual emotionally reacts to stressful situations.

Family relations

It is the participation in relationships, whether active or passive, within the family that provide the foundation for resilience to develop. Early attachments to close relatives and carers could provide the young child with their first opportunities to develop resilience. The carer who provides a child with a secure base from which to explore is providing the infant with an environment within which problems, challenges and stressors can be faced.

These early relationships provide the foreground to Erikson's (1959) theory of psychosocial development, which depicted that humans work through a series of life stages, in which they faced challenges. Success in facing these challenges equipped the individual to be able to face the next. The first four stages; trust versus mistrust, autonomy versus shame, initiative versus guilt, and industry versus inferiority all depict stressors, challenges and problems that enable the child to begin to develop resilience. They learn whether or not they can trust adults to cater to their needs, whether or not they are autonomous beings, how to set their own goals and work to achieve them, and how others achieve goals and solve problems.

As the child develops, parenting adjusts, effective parenting provides the young person with boundaries yet room to explore and build autonomy. The parent needs to protect, yet allow the young person to take risks. Parents need to teach children how to identify their own limits and to continue to provide a safe base from which to explore their world yet enable them to challenge and widen the scope of that world. However, early research into resilience by Cicchetti (2010), focused on the children of mothers with schizophrenia and Werner's (2000) study of children living in areas of high deprivation and low economic status showed that they thrived despite living in environments that placed them at high risk of low resilience and wellbeing. Therefore, we can conclude that there are other protective factors that should be taken into account when addressing how resilience develops.

Supportive environments

There are two forms of supportive environment; those based on social relationships with people and those based on built environments. Supportive environments offer an individual a sense of connection to the environment and with others who belong. A group of peers, a community, school and church potentially offer a supportive environment. A supportive environment could provide a child with an alternative attachment figure, warm close relationships with adults and peers and role models all of whom may provide opportunities to develop a sense of self as an autonomous, independent being. Equally these environments also provide opportunities to develop identity, sense of connectedness and cohesion through socialisation.

Warm and supportive relationships

A number of researchers have identified that the relationship between people supports the development of resiliency. A warm and supporting relationship (Masten, Herbers, Cutuli & Lafavor, 2010) that enables autonomy and intrinsic motivation to develop is ideal. Rogers (1992) identified core conditions that underpin this form of relationship, these being that the adult should maintain unconditional positive regard, demonstrate empathy and be congruent. In addition to these core conditions the style of communication impacts on decision-making and coping. Heron (2009) identified six types of interaction style; confrontative, prescriptive, informative, cathartic, catalytic and supportive. Adults in education settings will often prefer prescriptive styles, in which they offer a series of solutions to problems. While we may have a preferred style, we do need to consider amending and adjusting this in order to encourage our communication partner to make autonomous decisions.

Socialisation

Socialisation is the transmission of norms, values, ideas and behaviour patterns that enable the individual to develop social identities, by being part of a group they learn the norms and behaviours of the group. Socialisation provides the socially constructed blueprint for behaviour patterns such as the display of emotion in a public arena. Our social identities construct how an individual displays their emotional reactions; for example, in individualistic cultures it is expected that an individual portrays anger, whereas in collectivist cultures greater value is placed on harmony and cooperation within the culture, therefore public displays of emotion such as anger are minimal and discouraged. Likewise, historical constructions of gender identity have indicated differences in rules of the display of emotions.

Socialisation also provides the constructions of values and principles; for example, the values and principles of a professional teacher. We learn how to be a good teacher/pupil from being with likeminded others, as adults, as professionals. If our colleagues do not hold the same values as our own, or if an education provider does not match our vision on what education should be, we leave, due to the incongruence. In order to maintain our own wellbeing, we seek to gain consistence and congruence between ourselves and others, but also between our own values and principles and our actions. Incongruence leads to discomfort, which leads to stress and reduced wellbeing.

Returning to Rutter's (1987) work on protective factors, we are reminded that it is the interaction between the protective factors that provides a moderating impact on the person-stressor event. When one protective factor is challenged or missing, others provide support. Protective factors immunise against challenge and compensate for stressful events (Garmezy, Masten & Tellegen, 1984). When the stressor outweighs the protective factors, resilience could be viewed as lacking, waning or being under-utilised. It also increases the risk of a negative chain of events commencing in which low resilience or lack of coping leads to a negative outcome. This reinforces the individual's sense of low achievement, reducing motivation, increasing the likelihood of learned hopelessness developing, which Abraham, Metalsky and Alloy (1989) describe as an enduring expectation of failure and an expectation that a desirable outcome will not occur, and the chain, or spiral of negativity, continues. Alternate protective factors, if present, enable the individual or their social environment, to break the negative chain.

But how do we know if a person has these protective factors?

Resilience is not a fixed trait within an individual, it is a subjective sense of self, consequently it cannot be measured. However, a number of researchers have begun to measure the protective factors within an individual's sphere leading to an identification of their capacity to be resilient. These surveys, such as the Student Resilience Survey (SRS; Lereya et al., 2016) enable professionals to identify the position of gaps, potential points of risk or potential commencement points of negative chain reactions in an individual's protective factors.

The SRS measures a range of factors that promote positive outcomes, it contains 12 sub-scales that address external support, such as family, school and community connection, participation in home, school and community, and peer engagement and support, in addition to assessing internal factors such as self-esteem, empathy, goals and aspirations. In Lereya et al.'s (2016) study they found a negative correlation between many of these factors and emotional, behavioural and health problems, indicating that these are protective factors. However, the findings from this study, and others (Lereya et al., 2016; O' Connor, Berry, Lewis, Mulherin & Crisostomo, 2007) have indicated that high levels of empathy are positively related with emotional, behavioural and health problems.

Pause to reflect

Empathy is the ability to perceive, understand and share the emotions and thoughts of others. Why do you think high levels of empathy might be associated with emotional, behavioural and health problems?

As resilience is formed from interactions between the protective factors, it is not fixed and consequently cannot be blamed for lack of adaptation to a stressor; however, we can identify how an individual may react to a problem by looking at their previous experiences and behaviour patterns in relation to problems and specifically by looking at the patterns of coping skills (Masten, Gewirtz & Sapienza, 2013)

In this section we have developed a construction of resilience and identified a range of protective factors, in the next section we will look at how, in school, we can build protective factors, in order to support an individual's wellbeing, resiliency and coping strategies for stressors and hazards.

What can we do in the school environment?

In the school environment we are tasked with enabling the individual and their social environment to build and develop their protective factors. As Rutter (2006) suggests we are tasked with identifying the challenges, boosting protective factors and preparing the child for the future.

Pause to reflect

Thinking back to you own education:

- Identify examples of stressors and problems that you faced.
- Think about the phrases you have used to encourage someone to complete an action.
- Write a list of your expectations of children in your school.

Identifying the challenges

In today's classroom, children face a number of challenges, from making and maintaining friendships, feeling secure and safe within the environment, to stepping up to the cognitive challenges in the classroom and managing adults' expectations of their achievements and behaviours.

Meeting adult expectations

There are a number of challenges created by adults in education settings. These challenges have also been heard in staff meetings and therefore can be applied to the relationship between experienced and non-experienced educators. The following is not a complete list, in your reflections you can add your own, but they include;

- 'It was OK for me' – as an adult we need to be wary of how we place our own experiences and expectations on others, it is easy to reflect on our own education experiences and fall back to the premise, 'I survived, so they will have to too'. Perhaps we survived standing in front of our class and reciting poems/multiplication tables/reading aloud because of the interaction between our own protective factors?
- 'Do it for me' – another common failing is to prey on children's sense of required helpfulness (Rachman, 1979) in which we phrase success at tests as being beneficial to the teacher/school/the head.
- 'Good, but not good enough' – it is common practice to encourage children to edit and mark their own, and peers' work, in order to identify common mistakes and set themselves specific learning goals. While this is helpful in terms of developing literacy skills, the impact on the child is that they are regularly reminded that they are not good enough. For a child with a low sense of wellbeing or low expectancy of achievement, this could be the start of learned hopelessness'. It doesn't matter how hard they try, they won't be good enough', or indeed learned helplessness (see Seligman 1975); 'it is no good I just cannot get it right'.
- In secondary education, some schools will use the terms 'WWW' ('what went well') and 'EBI' ('even better if') as a means of communicating teacher expectations in an age-appropriate manner. While this encourages differentiation, and individualised learning goals, it also reinforces 'you are not good enough', particularly when then practice is performed from habit or school expectation, rather than with the young person from conscious reflection and conversation.

Labelling

There is a wealth of literature that addresses the benefits and limitations of labelling children. While for some it enables the identification of resources and alternative pathways through education, for those with identified mental health problems, or chronic stressors that may indicate they are at risk of low resilience, it means they can access individual and further support from professionals outside of the classroom. However; for some children, it isolates, highlights difference, limits or is used as a barrier to progression or as a means to prevent autonomy, control and connectedness. In relation to resilience, it is useful to identify whether the label leads to the commencement of a negative or positive chain of events.

Tracking

Pressure to track children from Key Stage 2 to GCSE and beyond is increasingly used as a measure to identify the performance of schools. In basic terms, it labels children and should be used with the same caution as labelling (see above). A child placed on a D/C or Level 4 grade GCSE track, with resilience, may over-achieve and can bathe in the glory of 'being cleverer than everyone thought'; however, what about those children who have fewer protective factors or who achieve as predicted? At the other end of the spectrum, what about the children identified as gifted and talented? How do they cope being on the receiving end of the pressure throughout secondary school of being on the track to achieve grade 9 across all subjects? The constant tracking and reporting cycle means that the child is constantly reminded of their worth.

In group, out group

A sense of cohesion with a community, such as a school, is a protective factor. According to Self Categorisation theory (see Turner, Hogg, Oakes, Reicher & Wetherll, 1987), once an individual joins a group/community and begins to identify similarities between themselves and the other members of the group, a social identity is born. However, for some adults, it is all too easy to prey on this sense of cohesion and identity in order to highlight breaches of behaviour norms, such as 'some of you are letting the side down', 'there are those of you who are not working enough' and 'some of you... you know who you are'. Statements such as these only serve to break down the cohesion or stimulate the formation of minority groupings.

The challenge to all in education is to become more aware of these phrases and actions, to critique their use. Linking this back to the challenge theory, it is not necessary to eradicate the phrases, but it is sufficient to question and note the benefits and challenges they pose to individuals.

Boosting it

There are numerous ways in which a school environment can boost the resiliency of its students and staff. Through providing specific input within the curriculum or as additional sessions for targeted individuals as well as through providing space and places for community cohesion to develop and through critique of the discourse used in the school.

Providing input

There are a wide range of inputs, training materials and books designed to increase students' resilience. Input lengths range from a hour-long session, such as the one designed by the Samaritans (2016) to introduce young people to coping strategies, to term long inputs, such as Hart, Blincow & Thomas' (2007) programme designed to build a resilient tutor group, which takes young people through the process of identifying basic needs through belonging, learning, coping and thinking about their core self. Regardless of the tool, the underpinning assumptions are that the classroom – and therefore the school community – is a place to build cohesion and coping skills, a place where children and young people can learn about emotions, develop their understanding of others, learn different methods to solve problems and learn how to overcome stressors.

However, in order to provide this input, the adult should have the same set of understandings, skills and resiliency in their own lives.

Pause to reflect

Think about yourself as educator:

- Who is in your support network?
- Who can you turn to?
- Are you integrated within your school/education team?
- Are you part of a collective?
- How do you overcome stressors?
- What coping skills do you utilise?
- What can you do to boost your own protective factors?

Outside of the classroom, schools can provide specialist input for those in need such as peer mentors. The school needs to offer easily identifiable points of contact for support on issues such as bullying. Time needs to be taken to identify who is the right person to lead these sessions, should it be an educational psychologist? Perhaps a specifically training teaching assistant, as identified by the ELSA programme (see Hills, 2008), or peers?

Space and place

Sports and other clubs/sessions are ideal opportunities to give young people the opportunity to meet and talk away from the formal classroom setting. By providing these spaces, a school is providing the pupils with opportunities to self-select support, to locate and identify others with similar interests and develop a sense of community based on those shared interests.

Space should also be provided for real discussion and inclusion in school decision-making and planning, many schools have 'student groups' that serve to influence school planning, but in order to boost resilience of the whole school community as well as the individuals within, these groups need to have direct impact, be a space of change and development and be valued by all within the community (see Chapter 3 of this book).

Not all spaces and places needs to have a specific focus. By providing space away from the classroom setting for talk, we are encouraging communication outside of education topics, a place to share emotions, ideas and thoughts, a place to locate a sense of self, rather than a name on a register or a label. An ideal activity for a student group might be to identify areas in the school where tables, chairs and other seating can be positioned to enable groups of young people to meet together and talk.

Discourse

Most schools have mission statements or statements of ethos; by framing these in a positive manner, outlining skills, strengths and goals, pupils and staff can focus on topics away from problems, develop shared communication on strengths and coping and increase connectiveness.

Likewise, in day-to-day communication, the focus should be on strengths and skills, moving away from reward and reinforcement as these encourage reliance on external motivation and behaviour that is conditional. Communication should be individualised, encouraging the young people to develop intrinsic motivation, to appreciate trial and error problem-solving, as this encourages continual trial to overcome obstacles and to make autonomous decisions.

Preparing

As previously mentioned, not all stressors can be planned and prepared for but we can prepare and plan to use coping strategies and resiliency when stressors occur, whether normative or non-normative.

Transitions

To support students in preparing for transitions, a number of activities could be introduced, from providing positive information about the changes about to occur to providing points and places for conversation and discussion.

Schools could open their doors to opportunities offered by other education providers, from secondary schools running sports events for all local primary school children, to visits from pre-schoolers to university settings.

Boundaries

Within the school, clear behavioural boundaries, not associated with a reward or punishment system, allow children to make autonomous and informed choices about their behaviour.

Removing the taboo

In many communities, certain topics are labelled as taboo. There are other topics that we feel are too sensitive or personal to discuss, or claim that the topics are not relevant for discussion with those under 18 years of age. But without openness and discussion, how are we to help individuals going through loss or bereavement? How do we help a student who has a parent who is deployed abroad in times of war? As adults in education, we need to consider how we talk about death, loss, deployment, sexual and other topics, which will enable our children to understand, prepare for potential stressors and seek to use their coping skills when faced with one of these non-normative stressors or transitions.

Section summary

In this section we have looked at the various approaches professionals can take to boost and prepare children for stressors, whether normative or non-normative. We have also begun to look at the common practices and phrases we use in education settings, which, while aiming to engender achievement and reach goals and targets, may in fact be having a negative impact on children's sense of wellbeing and resilience.

Chapter summary

Wellbeing and resilience are two related factors; while wellbeing is an individual's subject sense of happiness, satisfaction and meaning in life, resilience refers to the mechanisms they use to overcome hazards and risks. Both concepts are socially constructed. When we are considering resilience we need to focus on an individual's protective factors, and how these can be utilised or boosted to enable individuals to deal with hazards and risks to their wellbeing. In education we also need to think about how we provide risks and hazards to children's wellbeing, and the opportunities we provide them to have autonomy, control, choice and connectiveness. Equally importantly we need to consider our own wellbeing, to reflect on our own protective factors and to identify the hazards and risks that may challenge us, our professional values and the community in which we work.

References

Abramson, L.Y., Metalsky, G.I. & Alloy, L.B. (1989) Hopelessness depression: a theory-based subtype of depression. *Psychological Review*, 96, 358-372.
Brantley, A., Huebner, E. & Nagle, R. (2002) Multidimensional life satisfaction reports of adolescents with mild mental disabilities. *Mental Retardation*, 40(4), 321-329.

Cicchetti, D. (2010) Resilience under conditions of extreme stress: a multilevel perspective. *World Psychiatry: Official Journal of the World Psychiatric Association*, 9(3), 145–154.

Collin-Verzina, D., Daigneault, I. & Herbert, M. (2013) Lessons learned from child sexual abuse research: Prevalence, outcomes and preventative strategies. *Child and Adolescent Psychiatry and Mental Health*, 7(1), 1–22.

Department of Education (2016) *Mental Health and Behaviour in Schools: Departmental Advice for School Staff*. London: DoE.

Department of Health and NHS England (2015) *Future in Mind: Promoting, Protecting and Improving Our Children and Young People's Mental Health and Wellbeing*. London: DoH.

Diener, E. (2009) *The Science of Well-Being: The Collected Works of Ed Diener*. New York: Springer-Verlag.

Diener, E., Lucas, R. & Oishi, S. (2002) Subjective well-being: the science of happiness and life satisfaction, in *Handbook of Positive Psychology*. Oxford: Oxford University Press.

Erikson, E. (1959) *Identity and the Life Cycle: Selected Papers*. Oxford: International Universities Press.

Fell, F. & Hewstone, M. (2015) *Psychological Perspectives on Poverty*. York: Joseph Rowntree.

Garmezy, N., Masten, A.S. & Tellegen, A. (1984) The study of stress and competence in children: a building block for developmental psychopathology. *Child Development*, 55(1), 97–111.

Gilman, R., Easterbrooks, S. & Frey, M. (2004) A preliminary study of multi-dimensional life satisfaction among deaf/hard of hearing youth across environmental settings. *Social Indicators Research*, 66(1), 143–164.

Hart, A., Blincow, S. & Thomas, H. (2007) *Resilient Therapy: Working with Children and Families*. London: Routledge.

Heron, J. (2009) *Helping the Client: A Creative Practical Guide*. London: Sage.

Hills, R. (2008) An evaluation of the emotional literacy support assistant (ELSA) project from the perspectives of primary school children. *Educational & Child Psychology*, 33(4).

Jennings, P.A. & Greenberg, M.T. (2009) The pro-social classroom: teacher social and emotional competence in relation to student and classroom outcomes. *Review of Educational Research*, 79(1), 491–525.

Jutte, S., Bentley, H., Tallis, D., Mayes, J., Jetha, N., O'Hagan, O. & McConnell, N. (2015) *How Safe Are Our Children? The Most Comprehensive Overview of Child Protection in the UK*. London: NSPCC.

Kidger, J., Stone, T., Tilling, K., Brockman, R., Campbell, R., Ford, T. & Gunnell, D. (2016) A pilot cluster randomised controlled trial of a support and training intervention to improve the mental health of secondary school teachers and students – the WISE (Wellbeing in Secondary Education) study. *BMC Public Health*, 16(1), 1060.

Lazarus, R.S. & Folkman, S. (2009) *Stress, Appraisal and Coping*. New York: Springer.

Lereya, S.T., Humphrey, N., Patalay, P., Wolpert, M., Böhnke, J.R., Macdougall, A. & Deighton, J. (2016) The student resilience survey: psychometric validation and associations with mental health. *Child and Adolescent Psychiatry and Mental Health*, 10.

Lupien, S., King, S., Meaney, M. & McEwen, B.S. (2001) Can poverty get under your skin? Basal cortisol levels and cognitive function in children from low and high socioeconomic status. *Development and Psychopathology*, 13(3), 653–676.

Mani, A., Mullainathan, S., Shafir, E. & Zhao, J. (2013) Poverty impedes cognitive function. *Science*, 341, 976–980.

Masten, A.S., Gewirtz, A.H. & Sapienza, J.K. (2013) Resilience in development: the importance of early childhood, in *Encyclopedia of Early Childhood Development*. Available at http://www.child-encyclopedia.com/resilience/according-experts/resilience-development-importance-early-childhood.

Masten, A.S., Herbers, J.E., Cutuli, J.J. & Lafavor, T.L. (2010) Promoting competence and resilience in the school context. *Professional School Counseling*, 12(2), 76–84.

Mathiesen, K., Tambs, K. & Dalgard, O. (1999) The influence of social class, strain and social support on symptoms of anxiety and depression in mothers of toddlers. *Social Psychiatry and Psychiatric Epidemiology*, 34(2), 61–72.

Mellor, D.J. (2007) *Working Paper 88 Everyday and Eternal Acts: Exploring Children's Friendships in the Primary School*. Cardiff: Cardiff University.

Norton, D. (1976) *Personal Destinies*. Princeton: Princeton University Press.

NSPCC (2014) *Children in Care Statistics*. Available at http://bit.ly/1KJij34%0AOffice.

O'Connor, L.E., Berry, J.W., Lewis, T., Mulherin, K. & Crisostomo, P.S. (2007) Empathy and depression: the moral system on overdrive, in T.F.D. Farrow and P.W.R. Woodruff (eds.), *Empathy in Mental Illness*. New York: Cambridge University Press.

Rachman, S. (1979) The concept of required helpfulness. *Behaviour Research and Therapy*, 17(1), 1–6.

Roffey, S. (2012) Pupil wellbeing – teacher wellbeing: Two sides of the same coin? *Educational and Child Psychology*, 29(4), 8–17.

Rogers, C. (1992) The necessary and sufficient conditions of therapeutic personality change. *Journal of Consulting and Clinical Psychology*, 60(6), 827–832.

Rutter, M. (1987) Psychosocial resilience and protective mechanisms. *American Journal of Orthopsychiatry*, 57(3), 316–323.

Rutter, M. (2006) Implications of resilience concepts for scientific understanding. *Annals of the New York Academy of Sciences*, 1094, 1–12.

Samaritans (2016) Building Resilience. Available at www.samaritans.org.

Savage, M. (2017) Almost a quarter of teachers who have qualified since 2011 have left profession. *The Guardian*, 8 July. Available at www.theguardian.com/education/2017/jul/08/almost-a-quarter-of-teachers-who-have-qualified-since-2011-have-left-profession.

Siegel, D.J. (2014) *Brainstorm: The Power and Purpose of the Teenage Brain*. Victoria: Scrib.

Seligman, M. (1975) *Helplessness; On Depression, Development and Death*. Bedford: W.H. Freeman.

Suldo, S. & Shaffer, E. (2008) Looking beyond psychopathology: the dual-factor model of mental health in youth. *School Psychology Review*, 37(1), 52–68.

Turner, J.C., Hogg, M.A., Oakes, P.J., Reicher, S.D. & Wetherell, M.S. (1987) *Rediscovering the Social Group: A Self-Categorization Theory*. Oxford: Basil Blackwell.

UNICEF (n.d.) *Behind Closed Doors: The Impact of Domestic Violence on Children*. Available at www.unicef.org/media/files/Behind-ClosedDoors.pdf.

Werner, E. (2000) Protective factors and individual resilience, in J. Shonkroff & S. Meisels (eds.), *Handbook of Early Childhood Intervention*. Cambridge: Cambridge University Press.

8 Safeguarding

Rights and relationships

Chris Simpson

Introduction

'Safeguarding is everyone's responsibility' (HM Govt, 2015, p. 9). Those working in the high-pressure environment of schools may feel that this adds yet another burden to their responsibilities, but this chapter will show how good safeguarding practice can be incorporated in many mainstream features of school functioning and practice. The chapter does not provide details of the types of child abuse often encountered; neither does it give details of national or local processes and procedures involved in safeguarding, because these are constantly being revised. It is important that you are familiar with the safeguarding policy and processes of the school in which you work, and that you make sure this knowledge is up to date.

Safeguarding does not necessarily involve specialist knowledge but can involve many aspects of school life; thus, whether you are a student or an experienced teacher this discussion will provide opportunities for reflection on how, within your current role, you can contribute to creating and maintaining an effective safeguarding culture. This chapter will set the wider context for safeguarding in society and explain the distinction between safeguarding and child protection. It will then go on to argue for a rights-based approach to safeguarding in schools and explain how the concepts of risk and resilience can help schools actively promote the welfare of all their pupils. Later it explores some of the dimensions of 'relational practice' and argues that such practice is fundamental in terms of involving all staff in noticing when children may need additional support of some kind. Finally, it identifies how day-to-day interactions at school can play an important part in safeguarding pupils, and suggests that no matter how much or how little power and influence you have as a staff member, there will be opportunities for you to make improvements in safeguarding practice. Throughout, the focus is on under-18s, and although for simplicity the term 'children' is used, it is intended that the focus equally includes young people.

> **By the end of the chapter you will:**
>
> • Have developed your understanding of some of the principles and practices that underpin a robust, relationship-based approach to safeguarding all pupils.
> • Have considered the role that you as teacher can develop to promote safeguarding practices both within your own class and within the wider school.
> • Have an understanding of how important whole school ethos and culture is in providing a safe and secure environment for the child.

What is safeguarding?

Safeguarding can be defined as 'the process of creating a safe environment for the whole younger generation, as well as protecting those children and young people who are vulnerable or have already been harmed' (Lindon, 2008, p.15). It may be helpful to think of safeguarding as a continuum: at one end, are the majority of children and young people about whom there are no special concerns at this time, and at the other are children who may have experienced significant harm, or be at risk of doing so, about whom there are child protection concerns. Towards the middle, we might place children who are receiving one or more specialist interventions. At the child protection end of the continuum we would expect to see statutory services such as social care and the police involved. This paradigmatic view of safeguarding being a process relevant to the welfare and thriving of all children and all those who work with children came about in the UK as part of New Labour's Children Act of 2004 with its raft of measures relating to the 'Every Child Matters' agenda. This concept of safeguarding aims to put the child and their family at the centre with services configured around them. All children will be provided with 'universal' or 'population-based' services such as education and primary health care. If additional needs emerge, other services may be brought in: often as a result of a Common Assessment Framework (CAF) assessment. This means that *interprofessional working* and information-sharing underpin safeguarding processes especially as these move towards child protection.

Safeguarding is a universal process for all children: child protection will be needed for a small percentage of children and young people to the far right of the continuum (Figure 8.1). Early intervention will help to prevent children from moving closer to needing child protection.

Schools are one component of children's universal services and will regularly engage with children and young people who may be placed anywhere along this safeguarding continuum. Schools must comply with the current statutory guidance, and will have a safeguarding policy that all staff should

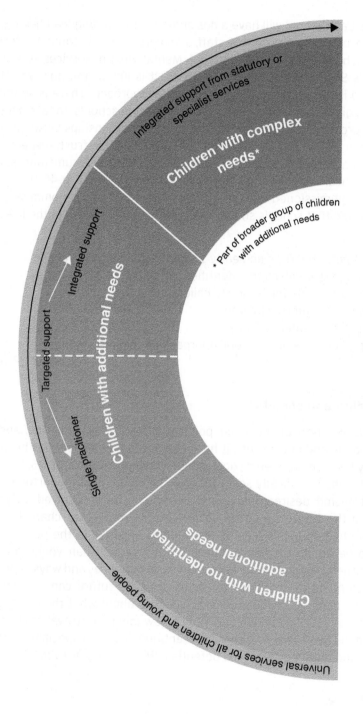

Figure 8.1 Processes and tools to support children and families (CWDC, 2009)
Diagram is not to scale in representing the proportion of children and young people in each section of the windscreen.

understand. Each school will have a designated safeguarding lead person, to whom concerns will be reported by staff, and this person will contact external agencies such as Child and Adolescent Mental Health Services (CAMHS) or Children's Social Care as the need arises. It is important, however, that safeguarding is not *dominated* by a procedural approach. There is so much opportunity, given the regular face-to-face contact in schools, to take a more nuanced approach to the whole child and to build relationships between children and their peers, and children and staff, which enable trust, respect and the ability to notice and respond to changes in children's circumstances; the 'embodied concern' identified by Peckover and Trotter (2015, p. 402).

A study commissioned by the Office of the Children's Commissioner (OCC) identified that schools should use their 'unique position in the lives of children' to

- spot potential risks and early signs and indications of abuse
- manage risks which are identified
- promote safety messages to children
- advise and inform children
- target early interventions
- implement a 'whole school' approach to children's wellbeing.

(OCC, 2012, p. 11)

Safeguarding and society

Schools are also part of the wider political and societal landscape, and in times of change and uncertainty, it has been noted that society has become particularly focused on, even anxious about, childhood (Jenks, 2005; Parton, 2017). Politicians specifically seem to view childhood as an opportunity for adults to transmit desired values and behaviours, often centred on compliance, into the future (Hendrick, 2016). This is sometimes characterised in terms of children being seen as apprentices engaged in the business of learning to be adults (James & James, 2008), rather than young human beings with their own distinctive perspectives, experiences and ways of being. The understanding of childhood-as-predictor-of the-future can be seen to operate like a magnet for more general anxieties about what the future has in store for our society, and we may notice how media portrayal of children often characterises them as either innocent/angelic, or – especially as they grow older and more powerful – as potentially threatening or even evil.

Media influence

Instances of child abuse provide the media with an opportunity to produce attention-grabbing stories of spectacular failings in child protection; for example, the iconic cases of Victoria Climbié and Peter Connelly ('Baby P') have been fully exploited and sensationalised by the media. At the same time, the perspectives and lived experience of children themselves is rarely attended to. The popular media provides compelling accounts involving innocent children and predatory monsters, which seem to be designed to shock, outrage and engender a strong desire for punishment and revenge. The public are provided with what Hendrick (2016, p. 247) calls a 'cocktail' of 'adult-centric narratives involving innocence, nostalgia, vulnerability, abuse and sentimentality'. This creates a climate of public outrage and politicians feel obliged to react by promising that failures in child protection will never happen again. The few cases of child abuse and killing that have a high media profile (for many others are not widely publicised) may influence governments to make changes to national safeguarding policy. For example, the Every Child Matters legislative framework was shaped by a variety of influences including research findings (DoH, 1995) but is also closely associated with the 2003 Laming enquiry into the Climbié case. Often the media will identify individuals who are blamed and scapegoated; these figures are publicly vilified and shamed (Jones, 2014). The popular media do not acknowledge the uncertainty and complexity that lies at the heart of child protection practice. Their narratives are unhelpful when needing to attend to our own responsibilities around safeguarding.

Pause to reflect

- Can you explain how child protection differs from safeguarding?
- What comes to mind when you think about your role in safeguarding children?
- Has your view been affected by media accounts of child protection failures and child deaths?
- Is there any action you can take to improve your confidence around your own role in safeguarding?

It is possible, especially when working in a general climate of defensive practice where professionals may be very concerned to 'cover their own backs', to focus on following procedure at the expense of keeping focused on the child. Munro (2011) in her review of social work practice commissioned by the UK government following the death of 'Baby P', advocated a re-focusing of practice away from the procedural approach. She found (p. 6) that 'the demands of bureaucracy have reduced [social workers'] capacity to work directly with children, young people and families' and reminded us that 'helping children is a human process. When the bureaucratic aspects of the task become too dominant, the heart of the work is lost' (p. 10). While statutory guidance and procedures must be followed, the quality of safeguarding will also be determined by the culture and ethos of the school, and the willing-ness of all staff to relate to children and to their families, in addition to having clear processes and procedures.

The role of schools

The challenge for schools is to deal competently with everyday aspects of safeguarding, from the universal promotion of the welfare of all children set out in Every Child Matters frameworks accompanying the Children Act (2004) to protecting children who are at risk of or are suffering from sig-nificant harm. It is estimated that about 10 per cent of children and young people may experience abuse at some time (Barlow & Scott, 2010). Policies of austerity tend to push resources further towards the child protection end of the continuum; however, prevention and early help are crucially important in safeguarding and there is a key role for schools here. Tarr, Whittle, Wilson and Hall (2013) point out that since children and young people spend around 169 days per year in school, school staff are ideally placed to notice signs or changes in their pupils that could indicate that they may be experiencing, or be at risk of experiencing, abuse or neglect.

Schools are engaging daily in face-to-face work with children, but many of the challenges faced by families will be beyond the influence of the school. Powell and Scanlon (2015) ask whether public scapegoating of individuals in safeguarding scandals may deflect attention from significant structural issues impacting on society as a whole. Butler and Drakeford (2008) and Parton (2014) agree that while 'scandal politics' attached to high-profile child protection failures play out in the media spotlight, wider concerns at a societal level such as poverty, poor mental health, insecure employ-ment and housing, are ignored. Poverty and related variables do not dir-ectly cause child abuse and neglect, but they do have an influence through placing greater stress on family life (Bywaters et al., 2016). There is also evidence showing that families from disadvantaged backgrounds are more likely to be subject to social care interventions. Child abuse and neglect occur in all strata of society, but professional parents have more social and educational capital and are less likely to be subject to investigation; we need to remember that those who neglect or abuse children will sometimes be professional people. Such people do not conform to commonly held stereo-types, and it may be easier to dismiss concerns about them rather than to investigate further (Bywaters et al., 2016)

In schools you will be working in accordance with current national legisla-tion and guidance on safeguarding children, and your school will have its own policy on safeguarding. The following sections aim to provide you with food for thought on approaches to safeguarding in the setting where you work and will argue that safeguarding is not an add-on, but an intrinsic part of the culture of your school.

Summary

- Safeguarding involves promoting the welfare of every child; a minority of children will also need child protection at some stage.
- We should be aware that media portrayal of child protection failures is often sensationalised.
- Schools are uniquely placed to play a part in safeguarding their pupils through everyday practice.

From paternalism to participation

Children are often conceptualised in terms of a 'deficit approach' that focuses on their needs and may not take account of their strengths. This perspective was fundamentally challenged by the United Nations Convention on the Rights of the Child (UNCRC) of 1989, which legislated globally for children's rights and their greater 'participation' in society. The Children Act of the same year established that in the UK 'the welfare of the child is paramount' and that children's views and wishes should be taken very much into account when decisions are being taken that will affect their lives. A 'new sociology of childhood' (Prout & James, 1997) emerged, emphasising that children were active agents in society with a unique insight into the lived experience of childhood, so concluding that children are 'experts in their own lives' (Langsted, 1994).

This view asserts that children should be protected not because they are helpless, but because they are human beings with rights, and this fundamentally includes the right not to be neglected or abused. Brooker advocated for *'Letting children speak* – because it is their right; because they are competent members of their social group, and because they contribute in important ways to their immediate environment' (2011, p. 140, emphasis in original).

Traditional approaches to safeguarding children tend to take a paternalistic approach based on the notion that adults are positioned to know what is best for children and will also act in their best interests. This approach, dubbed the 'caretaker perspective' by Dillen (2006, p. 237) constructs children as being essentially innocent, weak and vulnerable, and therefore in need of protection by wiser and more knowledgeable adults who are experienced in the ways of the world. Dillen draws on the writing of the Belgian academic Marc Depaepe to describe how through the process of 'pedagogisation: a kind of keeping children *little*, placing them on a pedestal, which invokes the image of a special *child island*' (2006, p. 243, emphasis added). This can characterise children not as worthy of respect, but rather as essentially dependent in their need to be cared for. While children do indeed require some protection, and provision of everyday necessities, they should also be granted the right of participation in matters that concern and impact upon their own lives. To deny this participation is to impose a paternalism that will deny their agency. Bath (2013) argues that our understandings of education and care need to be reconnected, and that in this process, children and adults should engage together in democratic practices.

Democracy and children's agency

By 'agency' we mean that a person of whatever age has the capacity to 'act on their own situations... to shape their own circumstances and ultimately achieve change' (Jeffrey, 2011, p. 6). A sense of agency empowers individuals to care for themselves and for others, to speak out and to understand that their actions in the world have meaning. Some experts argue that children should be regarded as citizens of their country (IAWGCP, 2007); Powell and Scanlon (2015, p. 265) assert: 'The voice of the child is fundamental to good child protection practice... Child citizenship needs to be constitutionally acknowledged in a democratic society.' It might be argued that children who are being trained to be docile and passive are being made more vulnerable to abuse.

Many schools have a School Council where democratically elected pupil representatives are involved and consulted on the running of the school. This sort of children's 'participation' can be meaningful or tokenistic to varying degrees – see various models of participation including Hart's (1992). The roots of democracy in education are long-established (Dewey, 1916) and have been maintained through the progressive education sector. It is difficult to envision a more effective way of learning, through experience, about democracy and citizenship. However, the tokenistic use of a School Council will effectively demonstrate to pupils that while the managers of the school seek their opinions, they will not actually take them seriously. This is often the case when these views challenge existing authority and structure. Therefore, there may be little point in engaging in the democratic process if the council is viewed in this tokenistic way. A representative School Council, on the other hand, whose views are taken seriously will foster responsibility, respect for a range of views and an understanding of the responsible exercise of democratic rights and processes. Pupils will gain a sense of ownership of policies if their views have been sought and taken into account, and may develop a school-wide shared understanding of issues such as bullying (OCC, 2012).

Commentators such as Kennedy (2006) argue that ingrained discrimination against children in society constitutes 'adultism'. If we look at those children who not only are denied their rights, but are subjected to apparently random acts of unkindness or abuse, we can see how they might fall into a position of 'learned helplessness', feeling that this treatment is bound to continue no matter what they do. This can be a precursor to developing depression, among other long-term ill-effects. Conversely, it is beneficial for children to learn that their actions do have an effect in the world: that they have agency and can make changes. It is, therefore, beneficial for children and young people to participate in a genuine power-sharing forum or to be consulted in other ways, as this allows them to use their agency and self-efficacy, and can enable them to have a stake how their school is run. Brooker (2011, p. 140) asserts that 'children are active social agents who contribute to the construction of the settings they attend', that is, they influence how their settings are thought of and understood by a range of stakeholders. School could be a place of compulsion and coercion; or alternatively offer a supportive and stimulating environment where children feel safe to explore, develop and express their views while at the same time attending to the views of others.

Pause to reflect

- How does your school enable pupils to participate in shaping its ethos?
- How could your own practice develop pupils' sense of their own agency?
- What implications might the message 'always do as you're told' have for safeguarding?

Making good use of children's strengths

Studies show that children often actively help when their families experience trauma such as domestic violence. Research has found that many child refugees have been reluctant to accept the designation of victimhood; when separated from parents, they may form peer support networks (Orgocka, 2012) or, if together with parents, provide emotional and physical support for them. Often children take on responsibilities when parents or siblings suffer from physical or mental ill-health. This illustrates how children can simultaneously be vulnerable and exercise power. Denying the power they have is likely to render them more vulnerable. Houghton's (2015) research found that although adults may not fully comprehend how difficult it is for a child to speak out about domestic abuse, abused children's participation in decision-making can be a powerful therapeutic tool. On a strategic level, it is widely advocated that children as users of services such as health and social care should be consulted when such services are commissioned and designed by local authorities; this is known as co-production. It can also be beneficial if children are consulted when school initiatives are being planned. Some schools whose safeguarding practices have been identified as outstanding (OCC, 2012) annually survey their students using a questionnaire to enquire into bullying and other areas of children's experience relevant to safeguarding.

Summary

- Children and young people will have a unique insight into their own lived experience.
- Schools can benefit from engaging in a range of democratic processes.
- Pupils have valuable insights that can improve school functioning;

Risk and resilience

Adverse experiences in childhood, such as neglect, trauma, abuse and loss can have a lifelong impact on individuals' physical and mental health and functioning in society. Stress and poor mental health impact adversely on pupils' ability to concentrate, their attendance and behaviour; underlying chronic child poverty is likely to compound these difficulties (Roffey, 2016). A report published by Public Health England (2015) found that:

> In an average class of 30 15-year-old pupils, three could have a mental disorder, ten are likely to have witnessed their parents separate, one could have experienced the death of a parent, seven are likely to have been bullied and six may be self-harming.

Researchers have tried to understand how it is that some children come through adverse experiences without experiencing serious ill-effects while others are more troubled as adults. Many identify a number of 'risk' factors alongside 'resilience' factors that are understood to have a protective effect. Risks can include having a learning disability, academic failure, school exclusion, conflict at home, loss of friendship or bereavement, bullying or being bullied, poor pupil–teacher relationships, witnessing domestic abuse or being subject to abuse, neglect or discrimination. Protective factors might include having high self-belief, having religious or spiritual faith, authoritative (not authoritarian) parenting, having a trusted and consistent adult figure in their life, a positive school culture, being emotionally aware and achieving well at school (Hanson & Holmes, 2014; Roffey, 2016; Department for Education, 2016; Beckett, Holmes & Walker 2017). The school has an opportunity to contribute significantly to its pupils' resilience through offering an 'oasis of safety' (OCC, 2012, p. 13). Support should be provided to pupils who need it as soon as possible in order to promote resilience (Beckett et al., 2017) and it may be appropriate to discuss with children what they would find helpful, thus enabling them to participate actively in their own safeguarding process (Koubel, 2016).

Roffey (2016, p. 33) identifies the following ways in which schools can support pupils' resilience:

- having high expectations combined with clear and consistent boundaries;
- providing opportunities to participate in and contribute to school life;

- teaching social and emotional skills such as cooperation, effective communication and problem-solving;
- supporting children's agency;
- working collaboratively with families;
- providing caring, positive adult role models.

Roffey (2016, p. 38) also asserts that 'Every interaction becomes an opportunity to promote resiliency'.

Pause to reflect

Identify examples of your own individual practice and whole-school practices that are supporting pupils' resilience. Are there further actions you could take?

Summary

- Children will have a mix of risk and resilience factors in their lives; this balance will change at different points in time.
- Schools can play a key role in strengthening the resilience of all children.
- Specialist skills are not needed to support resilience.

Relational practice

Most children will have a trustworthy adult in their family, but if they do not, school may be the environment where they look for somebody to fulfil this crucial role. Such an adult will convey a sense of belief in the positive potential of the young person or child and is likely to take their concerns seriously.

Teaching assistants and other support staff are well-positioned to form caring relationships with their pupils and it is important that the school hierarchy takes the views of non-teaching staff seriously, particularly when safeguarding is concerned.

The importance of relationships in building a positive school culture is fundamental, and we need to think about this in terms of the whole school community. If there is bullying in the staffroom, then we should not be surprised to find it rife among pupils as well. It is important that pupils feel confident enough to take their worries to other pupils or to staff (including non-teaching staff). Studies identifying outstanding practice in safeguarding (OCC, 2012, 2013) have found that pupil peer mentoring at primary and secondary schools can have benefits in contributing to an atmosphere of trust, safety and empowerment, although at the same time thought must be given to providing immediate support if distressing disclosures are made by children to their peers.

Much has been written about the process of 'listening' to children and enabling their 'voice' to be heard; this can take place through formal processes of consulting with children as described earlier, but is perhaps even more important through everyday practice of face to face contact. Brooker (2010, p. 183) cites Nodding's (2002) notion of care as 'receptive attention' and explains how both the caregiver and the cared-for person contribute to the relationship, and both gain from it. We can probably all recall an example where we felt good because we had been able to give hope or inspiration to a child with whom we were working; indeed, it may be that the rewards we get from teaching, and playing a part in children's positive development, provide the motivation that keeps us working as teachers.

Noticing

The behaviour of children and young people can be a good indicator of their wellbeing or, alternatively, their distress; therefore, noticing changes in behaviour is one of the key ways in which safeguarding concerns may be first identified. Violent behaviours may be indicative of violence at home; age-inappropriate sexualised behaviour may be indicative of sexual abuse. Lateness, sleepiness and uncompleted homework can be a consequence of children having caring responsibilities at home, which are impacting on their wellbeing. Inability to concentrate can result from suffering trauma. Teachers will be under pressure to meet performance targets and so understandably find such behaviours challenging and stressful, but it is worth taking the time to investigate and respond appropriately in order that the action taken is more likely to be effective in promoting a positive outcome. Withdrawn behaviour, although it may not present challenges to classroom management, should also alert us to potential problems in or out of school.

Staff training should raise awareness that challenging or withdrawn behaviour, or a pattern of lateness or absence from school is often a presenting symptom of difficulty or distress in another area of the child's life; and that noticing changes in the way children look and behave – what Peckover and Trotter (2015, p. 402) term 'embodied recognition' – can be an effective means of identifying potential safeguarding issues. 'Pastoral support relies on a high degree of attentiveness. If we know our students, we can also respond to our gut feeling if something is wrong' (SENCO in OCC, 2013, p. 42)

Modelling

Mutually respectful relationships involving staff members, pupils and families take time to build and care to maintain. Staff are potential positive role models, particularly where adult behaviour out of school is unpredictable, aggressive or neglectful, and it is important that staff are able to keep to codes of behaviour that are expected of pupils.

Pause to reflect

- Recall an example of 'receptive attention' when you were able to care for a pupil – and both of you gained from this.
- Notice how a range of school staff relate to pupils. What attitudes and behaviours are being modelled?

Summary

- Schools benefit from respectful and reciprocal relationships at all levels.
- The school ethos should be evident in everyday interactions.
- Challenging or withdrawn behaviour can be an indicator of distress.

Good practice in schools

Safeguarding involves every member of the school community, with each staff member and voluntary helper understanding what their role and responsibility is. Recruitment practices should signal from the outset that the school prioritises the safeguarding of its pupils and that safeguarding practices go above and beyond a procedural approach, extending to a concern for children's overall wellbeing. Support staff such as meal-time assistants, caretakers and bus drivers should be involved in safeguarding processes and training; interactions in the playground should be noticed. Children and indeed parents/carers may feel it easier to confide in a staff member whose role is perceived as caring rather than authoritative. It is often those staff working at the 'front line' who are best positioned to hear, see and notice what may be significant in terms of safeguarding. Any staff member or volunteer should feel able to raise concerns and know who to take these to. Safeguarding training should be regularly refreshed and staff who have participated in training will be well-placed to contribute to policy reviews.

Children may be reluctant to speak about problems such as domestic abuse, fearing that they will be identified as being 'different' and be vulnerable to ridicule or bullying (Buckley, Holt & Whelan, 2007; Spinney, 2013). They may also fear that if they disclose abuse, the situation will be taken out of their hands, and they will have no control over what happens next, thus experiencing another layer of disempowerment by adults. Schools should therefore consider being open about levels of confidentiality offered by staff (for example, a school nurse may work to a higher level of confidentiality than a class teacher), and where information does have to be passed on to other agencies, by sharing this appropriately with the child who has disclosed. Specialist agencies and confidential helplines such as ChildLine can also be publicised and this also sends a visible message that safeguarding is an issue that is important to the school.

Embedding safeguarding across teaching and care practices

Working with children who have been harmed can be distressing and one study showed that the typical process in schools was to aim to recognise signs of harm, and then refer and signpost to other specialist services (Peckover & Trotter, 2015) with little further thought to interventions put in place within the school. Increasingly, however, these external agencies have raised the 'thresholds' that must be met before their service can be accessed and may therefore ask for more 'evidence' before they can offer help. School staff should not underestimate the value to pupils of providing the possibility of a relationship with a trusted adult, a safe and consistent environment, and supportive friends – all of which can be found in a school that values all its members. Studies show that young carers and children who are experiencing domestic violence place a high value on 'normal activities', and the opportunity to talk and to share their feelings with somebody else (Buckley et al., 2007; Spinney, 2013).

Where there are child protection concerns, staff should take their concerns to the designated safeguarding lead within the school. Lesser concerns should also be reported, so that information can be pieced together to gain a fuller picture. Current government guidance is available on the internet, and organisations such as the NSPCC and the Office of the Children's Commissioner are good sources of further information and guidance on current best practice.

Pause to reflect

Children say that they need:

- Vigilance: to have adults notice when things are troubling them.
- Understanding and action: to understand what is happening; to be heard and understood; and to have that understanding acted upon.
- Stability: to be able to develop an ongoing stable relationship of trust with those helping them.
- Respect: to be treated with the expectation that they are competent rather than not.

(HM Govt, 2015)

The curriculum offers further opportunities for effective safeguarding practice. For example, sex and relationships education can address, in an age-appropriate fashion, issues of consent, emotional wellbeing, the exercise of power within relationships and sources of support. Staff should be aware of that around one-third of sexual abuse is committed by other children and young people (Hackett, Holmes & Branigan, 2016)and that children with disabilities are three times more likely to experience abuse than other children (Miller & Brown, 2014). These issues often feel very personal and private, and students may be unsure how to communicate their situation. It is important that staff delivering Relationships Education, Relationships and Sex Education and Personal, Social, Health and Economic Education are well-trained, confident and supported in these skilful roles. Online safety should also be incorporated in the curriculum. Children who are not educated about the risks of exploitation are left unprotected (Beckett et al., 2017), but schools can play a significant part in helping children to feel safe and also to keep themselves safe; and to have an appropriate language to use when communicating about such issues. Drama and role-playing can offer good opportunities for exploring some of these areas.

Case study

Bobbie is a pupil in your class who is currently in her final term before moving up to secondary school, where her sister is already a pupil. Her behaviour has recently become erratic, and when you confront her about increasingly regular late arrivals at school, she storms out of the room, crying and shouting that 'you're all the same and nobody understands!'

- What are your concerns?
- What actions would you take in relation to Bobbie?
- What is in place in the school where you work/have been on placement that would be potentially helpful?
- What actions could be taken by other staff at your school?
    See the Notes at the end of this chapter for a commentary

---

As mentioned above, children with disabilities and special educational needs experience statistically higher levels of abuse. It is particularly important that these children are supported and attention paid to changes in their behaviour. All children, including those with impairments, need to have a language to voice their concerns, and in some cases this language will be non-verbal.

Chapter summary

The following points are some of those that have been found by the Office of the Children's Commissioner to characterise good practice in primary schools (2012) and secondary schools (2013):

- School culture of open communication and respect.
- All staff receive regular training and understand how their role contributes to safeguarding.
- Strategic vision led by senior managers.
- Going above and beyond statutory requirements.

Notes on case study

You might be concerned that Bobbie's changed behaviour relates to adverse changes in circumstances at home or at school. It is possible that the impending transition to secondary school is relevant here.

Actions you might consider include: speaking to Bobbie when she is calmer and you have more privacy; asking colleagues whether they have noticed any changes; contacting a parent/carer and saying that you have some concerns

The school might have in place a peer support or buddy team, a designated person children can go to if they have worries, or a nurture group for children who are transferring to secondary school. A school culture where children are listened to and supported will underpin effectiveness.

Your designated safeguarding lead might have information from other staff relating to this girl or her family - here your information will add to the bigger picture. They might contact the secondary school to see if there are any concerns about Bobbie's sister.

References

Barlow, J. & Scott, J. (2010) *Safeguarding in the 21st Century: Where to Now?* Dartington: Research in Practice.

Bath, C. (2013) Conceptualising listening to young children as an ethic of care in early childhood education and care. *Children and Society*, 27, 361-371.

Beckett, H., Holmes, D. & Walker, J. (2017) *Child Sexual Exploitation: Definition and Guide for Professionals*. Dartington: Research in Practice.

Brooker, L. (2010) Constructing the triangle of care: power and professionalism in practitioner/parent relationships. *British Journal of Educational Studies*, 58(2), 181-196.

Brooker, L. (2011) Taking children seriously: an alternative agenda for research? *Journal of Early Childhood Research*, 9(2), 137-149.

Buckley, H., Holt, S. & Whelan, S. (2007) Listen to me! Children's experiences of domestic violence. *Child Abuse Review*, 16, 296-310.

Butler, I. & Drakeford, M. (2008) Booing or cheering? Ambiguity in the construction of victimhood in the case of Maria Colwell. *Crime, Media, Culture* 4(3), 367-386.

Bywaters, P., Bunting, L., Davidson, G., Hanratty, J., Mason, W., McCartan, C. & Steils, N. (2016) *The Relationship between Poverty, Child Abuse and Neglect: An Evidence Review*. London: Joseph Rowntree Foundation. Accessed at www.jrf.org.uk/report/relationship-between-poverty-child-abuse-and-neglect-evidence-review.

Children's Workforce Development Council (CWDC) (2009) *The Team around the Child (TAC) and the Lead Professional: A Guide for Managers*. Accessed at www.choiceforum.org/docs/leadpro.pdf.

Department for Education (2016) *Mental Health and Behaviour in Schools*. Accessed at www.gov.uk/government/publications/mental-health-and-behaviour-in-schools-2.

Dewey, J. (1916) *Democracy and Education*. New York: Macmillan.

Department of Health (DoH) (1995) *Child Protection: Messages from Research*. London: The Stationery Office.

Dillen, A (2006) Children between liberation and care: ethical perspectives on the rights of children and parent-child relationships. *International Journal of Children's Spirituality*, 11(2), 237-250.

Hackett, S., Holmes, D. & Branigan, P. (2016) *Operational Framework for Children and Young People Displaying Harmful Sexual Behaviours*. London: NSPCC.

Hanson, E. & Holmes, D. (2014) *That Difficult Age: Developing a More Effective Response to Risks in Adolescence*. Dartington: Research in Practice.

Hart, R. (1992) *Children's Participation from Tokenism to Citizenship*. Florence: UNICEF.

Hendrick, H. (2016) *Narcissistic Parenting in an Insecure World*. Bristol: Policy Press.

HM Govt (2015) *Working Together to Safeguard Children*. Accessed at www.workingtogetheronline.co.uk/chapters/intro.html.

Houghton, C. (2015) Young people's perspectives on participatory ethics: agency, power and impact in domestic abuse research and policy making. *Child Abuse Review*, 24, 235-248.

Inter-Agency Working Group on Children's Participation (IAWGCP) (2007) *Children as Active Citizens: A Policy and Programme Guide*. Accessed at https://resourcecentre.savethechildren.net/library/children-active-citizens-policy-and-programme-guide-commitments-and-obligations-childrens.

James, A. & James, A.L. (2008) *Key Concepts in Childhood*. London: Sage.

Jeffrey, L. (2011) *Understanding Agency: Social Welfare and Change*. Bristol: Policy Press.

Jenks, C. (2005) *Childhood*, 2nd ed. Abingdon: Routledge

Jones, R. (2014) *The Story of Baby P: Setting the Record Straight*. Bristol: Policy Press.

Kennedy, D. (2006) *The Well of Being: Childhood, Subjectivity and Education*. New York: SUNY Press.

Koubel, G. (2016) Constructing safeguarding, in G. Koubel (ed.), *Safeguarding Adults and Children: Dilemmas and Complex Practice*. London: Palgrave.

Laming, Lord (Department of Health) (2003) *The Victoria Climbié Inquiry: Report of an Inquiry by Lord Laming*. London: Department of Health.

Langsted, O. (1994) Looking at quality from the child's perspective, in P. Moss & A. Pence (eds.), *Valuing Quality in Early Childhood Services: New Approaches to Defining Quality*. London: Paul Chapman.

Lindon, J. (2008) *Safeguarding Children and Young People: Child Protection 0–18 Years*, 3rd ed. London: Hodder Education.

Miller, D. & Brown, J. (2014) *'We Have the Right to be Safe': Protecting Disabled Children from Abuse*. London: NSPCC. Accessed at www.nspcc.org.uk/globalassets/documents/research-reports/right-safe-disabled-children-abuse-summary.pdf.

Munro, E. (2011) *The Munro Review of Child Protection Final Report: A Child Centred System*. London: The Stationery Office.

Noddings, N. (2002) *Educating Moral People*. New York: Teachers College Press.

Office of the Children's Commissioner (OCC) (2012) 'You Have Someone to Trust': Outstanding Safeguarding Practice in Primary Schools. London: Office of the Children's Commissioner. Accessed at www.childrenscommissioner.gov.uk/sites/default/files/publications/You_Have_Someone_to_Trust.pdf.

Office of the Children's Commissioner (OCC) (2013) *Feeling Safe, Keeping Safe: Good Practice in Safeguarding and Child Protection in Secondary Schools*. London: Office of the Children's Commissioner. Accessed at www.childrenscommissioner.gov.uk/sites/default/files/publications/Feeling_safe_keeping_safe.pdf.

Orgocka, A. (2012) Vulnerable yet agentic: independent child migrants and opportunity structures, in A. Orgocka and C. Clark-Kazak (eds.), Independent Child Migration – Insights into Agency, Vulnerability and Structure. New Directions for Child and Adolescent Development, 136. New York: Wiley.

Parton, N. (2014) *The Politics of Child Protection:Contemporary Developments and Future Directions*. Basingstoke: Palgrave Macmillan.

Parton, N. (2017) Concerns about risk as a major driver of professional practice, in M. Connolly (ed.), *Beyond the Risk Paradigm in Child Protection*. London: Palgrave.

Peckover, S. & Trotter, T. (2015) Keeping the focus on children: the challenges of safeguarding children affected by domestic abuse. *Health and Social Care in the Community* 23(4), 399-407.

Powell, F. & Scanlon, M. (2015) *Dark Secrets of Childhood: Media Power, Child Abuse and Public Scandal*. Bristol: Policy Press.

Prout, A. & James, A. (1997) A new paradigm for the sociology of childhood? Provenance, promise and problems, in A. Prout & A. James (eds.), *Constructing and Reconstructing Childhood: Contemporary Issues in the Sociological Study of Childhood*. London: Routledge.

Public Health England (2015) *Promoting Children and Young People's Emotional Health and Wellbeing: A Whole School and College Approach*. Accessed at www.gov.uk/government/publications/promoting-children-and-young-peoples-emotional-health-and-wellbeing.

Roffey, S. (2016) Building a case for whole-child, whole-school wellbeing in challenging contexts. *Educational and Child Psychology*, 33(2), 30-42.

Spinney, A. (2013) Safe from the start? An action research project on early intervention materials for children affected by domestic and family violence. *Children and Society*, 27(5), 397-405.

Tarr, J., Whittle, M., Wilson, J. & Hall, L. (2013) Safeguarding children and child protection education for UK trainee teachers in higher education. *Child Abuse Review*, 22, 108-115.

9 Using critical reflective practice to develop and thrive as a teacher

Jan Gourd and MarkAndrew Dearden

During the late 1980s and 1990s, education in England saw changes with the introduction of the National Curriculum. Established from the Education Act (1988), it was subsequently altered and restructured through various reviews. It finally settled into the National Curriculum (1999), which would remain in place until the introduction of the new curriculum in September 2014.

Contemplating primary education during this time, Halstead noted that, 'schools and individual teachers within schools [were] a major influence... on the developing values of children and young people, and thus of society at large' (1995, p. 3).

If schools were to present a reflection of the values of society, the groups that made up society could be seen to be vying for influence and domination of curriculum content.

Halstead (1995) suggests that in the classrooms, teachers were feeling the pressure of curriculum changes taking place throughout the decade. Teachers presented children with values drawn from their personal positioning: embedded in their own worldview. Sometimes these values lacked critical reflection, maybe a result of poor training; or being so fully engaged in the job of teaching that values were based on moral instinct rather than being fully debated in a professional context but in a time of ideological flux and competition teachers needed to ask themselves what was important.

Halstead notes that where schools had seen the importance of values and values education, a value statement was produced, but this would have limited impact if teachers were not part of the 'creation' process and did not share an understanding of the meaning behind the statement. This is a point that is echoed by Brighouse (2006).

At the time of the creation of the National Curriculum, consideration of many key factors were important: a growing cultural diversity among school communities; a gulf opening between the values of teachers and the values of government; a perceived moral decline in children, and in wider public life;

and the determination of government to uphold certain values. Compliance to the National Curriculum would be achieved by subjecting schools to regular inspection via Ofsted. Among otherthings, Ofsted were tasked to comment on spiritual, moral, social and cultural education in the school.

At the turn of the century, Noddings (2003) contributed to a growing body of literature that problematised the neoliberal ideology that dominated teaching practice at this point. The issue of education being about something more than academic achievement is clear in her work.

Noddings (2006) argues for the development of a new type of professional or at the very least a recognition of the care ethic that should pervade our interpretation of professionalism. Noddings (2003, 2006) believes it is the caring teacher who goes beyond the legislative framework that can promote wellbeing, thriving and flourishing in the child. For Noddings (2003) the *in loco parentis* traditional conception of the teacher should be foregrounded. The teacher should embed within their professional role the care akin to that of the parent. Noddings (2003) suggests that happiness should be an aim of life and education. She suggests that we should educate children for personal life and public life and that in doing so we will enable individuals to thrive both personally and professionally:

> One purpose of schools should be to develop the intellect, but that does not mean to stuff the heads of children with material arbitrarily chosen by experts and designed to rank and sort them. It means rather to guide students towards the use of their intellectual faculties in both personal and public life.
>
> (Noddings, 2003, p. 260)

Noddings (2006) clearly acknowledges that life in the 21st century has changed and that parents – mothers specifically – no longer stay at home, affording the nurturing that children need. Schools now need to become like the best families to the child, and nurturing is very much part of that agenda, in fact more so than specific curricular objectives.

This then places a great burden on the teacher as they juggle the competing agendas of performativity and nurture. To thrive as a teacher, individuals need to develop a professionalism based on values that allow them to recognise what is of greatest importance to the child in their care and to be selective over what to give prominence to at any given point. This is professional judgement and the teacher who bases that judgement on well-defined principles is more likely to thrive as they will have the confidence and energy to defend their principles, to do the right thing. Energy wasted on not acting according to principles, causes the teacher stress and ultimately burnout.

By the end of the chapter you will:

- Have an understanding of the notion of critical reflective practice.
- Have considered your own professionalism.
- Have developed an understanding of how managing your own well-being and flourishing can help you avoid stress.

Using critical reflective practice to reconcile personal principles in professional work

Having looked at all the challenges that teachers face in their everyday lives, it is imperative that teachers develop strategies to help them thrive in their chosen profession.

Teacher stress and burnout affect 83 per cent of teachers according to a 2015 survey for the NASUWT (Precey, 2015). The reasons for that stress included workload, pupil behaviour and inspection.

In order to flourish we know that every individual needs to experience positive feelings and wellbeing. This has been conceptualised by numerous authors in different ways; for example, as stated by Watson, Emery and Bayliss (2012, p.1) the National Institute for Clinical Excellence defined well-being as encompassing

- Happiness, confidence and not feeling depressed (emotional wellbeing);
- A feeling of autonomy and control over one's life, problem-solving skills, resilience, and a sense of involvement with others (psychological wellbeing); and
- The ability to have good relationships with others and to avoid disruptive behaviour, delinquency, violence or bullying (social wellbeing).

Seligman (2012) suggests that in order to flourish a number of facets need to be in place. He calls this PERMA:

Personal Enjoyment: the pleasant life

Engagement: a flow state in which thought and feeling are usually absent;

(Positive) **R**elationships: relationships are key to the development of all humans;

Meaning: belonging to and serving something that is bigger than the self;
Accomplishment: the pursuit of success, achievement, and mastery for its own sake.

When any of the above are interrupted, then the individual is not thriving and often experiencing stress. Being able to isolate what is causing the stress means that individuals can seek to address those areas and move forward. Teachers often find this hard to do but unless stressors can be identified then it is hard to develop protectors and to develop professional resilience for the future. This chapter suggests that teachers first need to learn how to critically reflect on critical incidents in their professional lives and then need to isolate those aspects of incidents that challenged their wellbeing and ultimate flourishing.

Critical reflection

In initial training, teachers are taught to be reflective, to consider the strengths and weaknesses of their practice. In order to thrive, we need to take this one stage further and enable teachers to use critical reflective practice to develop their 'principled professionalism' (Goodson, 2000)

A good starting point for critical reflective practice is to look at critical incidents in our work. These critical moments being, 'vivid happenings that for some reason people remember as being significant' (Brookfield, 1995, p. 114). I often suggest to students that they look for 'penny-drop' moments; happenings that they remember because they illuminated an aspect of practice to the student, shone new light on something, they saw something anew. Critical incidents can also be events that caused us to feel uncomfortable, moments that interrupted the flow of our professional lives.

Having isolated the critical incident then that incident can be unpicked to isolate the specific antecedents, circumstances, assumptions and actions that made it critical. It is often understanding the complexity of the players, place, time and action/interaction that allow us to really understand the situation. Thinking this can help us to rationalise the incident and build strategies leading to resilience for the future.

Pacini-Ketchabaw (2015) suggest that critical reflective practice can allow the educator to develop ethically based possibilities in practice, to use their principles to enact their role as educator. This is very important when faced with situations that make us uncomfortable. Did I act according to the principles I hold dear? If so, then further analysis of the situation can reveal assumptions that were made both by oneself and by others and often the principled positions of the players will differ. This is what makes the incident a critical incident, somewhere at some point different principles were at play leading to differing assumptions. 'Critical reflective teaching happens when we identify and scrutinize the assumptions that undergird how we work' (Brookfield, 1995, p.xii)

Pacini-Ketchabaw (2015, p. 42) further suggest that all situations are part of a complex network and that reflection will involve 'assemblages of different matter'. They suggest that we should move to a more diffractive state of mind whereby we complexify our reflection in order to consider problems in a new light, to challenge and move forward developing new and stronger ways of working.

In order to make use of this notion, I intend to give some examples encountered throughout my career. I will work through these examples using frameworks to shape the thinking.

Scenario 1: student teacher on final placement

The critical incident

One evening, the parent of Paul comes into school and engages Mary in conversation about Paul. The conversation is very wide-ranging and veers onto the topic of Paul's written work. Mary has been especially pleased with Paul, he has worked well for her and has just produced a long and complex story that Mary considers shows very good ability in this area. She tries to allay the parent's concern and tells her that last year on teaching practice she had a Year 4 class and that Paul's work was as good as the majority of work from that class. The parent and Paul beam. On the way out of the school the parent bumps into the head teacher (who is also the class teacher) and tells her the good news. Rather than being pleased, the head teacher expresses surprise and the parent and Paul leave somewhat deflated. The head teacher then goes to find Mary and tells her that she has no right as a student to comment to parents about children's progress and that she should have referred such a question to her the substantive teacher.

In order to use this incident productively, the student needs to consider the various aspects of the incident critically. A good starting point is to look at the specific circumstances and then the many assumptions that are made in the scenario.

The circumstances here at first seem clear. They involve a student-teacher in what she believes to be an informal encounter with a parent of a child in her class. There is no tension until there is a chance encounter between the parent and the head teacher. Indeed, Mary is acting at all times according to her principles, she believes the child has tried hard and sees the child as capable.

There are assumptions made on the part of all the players and this is a good starting point for both learning about practice and developing resilience to overcome future problems. In analysing the incident, the student can develop the protectors for their own mental health (see Chapter 7).

Analysing the antecedents and circumstances

The main antecedent here was that after meeting with Mary the parent, by chance, bumped into the head teacher and wanted to share the positivity she felt Mary had towards her child's progress in writing.

Analysing the assumptions

In making sense of all the complexity of the situation we have to analyse the assumptions each person makes.

Parent assumptions

As Mary had been teaching the class pretty much full time for the past eight weeks, the parent had seen Mary in the role of class teacher and had trusted her with the education of her child. She had assumed that Mary was doing a pretty good job as she had seen her son progress over that time. She found Mary easy to talk to (maybe she was able to give the parent more time that the head teacher/class teacher who would be subject to other pressures).

She had incidentally raised the subject of Paul's writing, it was not the purpose of her visit to the class.

Mary's assumptions

As she had been in the school for eight weeks Mary had become very comfortable with her role. She liked the class and the school and she was viewed by the staff as doing an excellent job. She had felt very at ease talking to the parent and while she wouldn't have raised the issue of the pupil's writing, she did not feel that she was stepping out of place by responding intuitively to the parent's concern. She was very hurt and surprised by the head teacher's annoyance. She had forgotten that she was still a 'legitimate peripheral participant' in the school; that, is she was not a paid member of staff and had no 'legitimate' professional standing (Lave & Wenger, 1997)

The head teacher's assumptions

She felt that Mary should understand that she was not the class teacher and that she should remember that she would be gone next week and she, the head teacher, would have to pick up the class again. She was also slightly annoyed that she had had great difficulty in developing Paul's writing and had had many conversations about how difficult he found writing. She was not aware of the progress he had made with Mary. She felt that Mary should have told her that before sharing the information with a parent.

Table 9.1 Wellbeing: Mary

Wellbeing		
Emotional wellbeing (happiness, confidence, lack of stress)	Psychological wellbeing (autonomy, control, resilience, problem-solving skills, attentiveness, connectedness to others)	Social wellbeing (good relationships with others)
Mary's confidence in making assessments of children's progress was challenged.	Mary's sense of autonomy, what she could and couldn't do or say were compromised.	The knocking of Mary's confidence in the social relationships that she had built during her time at the school were the most disturbing to her.
Mary's confidence in interacting with parents was challenged.	Her relationship connectedness to all parties, the parent, the head teacher and the child, were put in difficulty.	She wondered how other professionals within the school would react when they heard about the incident.
Her confidence in how she was seen in the school was challenged (i.e., 'just a student').	Her principles of praising children when praise was deserved were disrupted.	

As you can see from this scenario, the incident has raised a number of emotions in each party and it is the playing out of those emotions that has made this a critical incident for Mary. Mary goes home feeling bad and can't get the events out of her head. By critically reflecting and analysing each person's assumptions Mary can hopefully rationalise what has happened, she will be able to put her feelings into perspective and maybe 'bounce back' more quickly without the incident clouding her last few days in the school and without damaging her relationships with the staff.

Table 9.1 provides us with further insight into Mary's wellbeing. It is clear that Mary had her confidence knocked. She was starting to feel like a real teacher in the school, that she had been accepted by the school community as a fellow professional and now she felt that she had misjudged the relationships. She also felt awkward that the head teacher had felt the need to put her in her place. She now doubted whether if she applied for the vacancy at the school she would be considered for the position and she also wondered if she now wanted to work in the school now anyhow as she began to doubt whether her own principles of positivity and celebration towards children when children made progress were shared across this school's community. Could she work in a school that did not seem to share her own

Table 9.2 Flourishing: Mary

Flourishing				
Personal Enjoyment	*Engagement-Flow*	*Relationships*	*Meaning*	*Accomplishment*
Her enjoyment of the next few days with the class were diminished.	The incident kept coming back to her replaying in her mind.	Her relationships with those in the school became less authentic and more guarded. She was careful about what she said and to whom. Others noticed that she didn't seem herself.	The meaning of her last few days in the school changed. She stopped seeing herself as potentially being employed at the school.	She felt that her accomplishments with the class were diminished. Many teachers had commented on her success in engaging the children in quality writing but her sense of pride in this now lacked authenticity.

personal beliefs and values about children? So the complexity of a seemingly small encounter produced a myriad collection of thoughts, feelings and subsequent possibilities for action.

In terms of her flourishing as a professional teacher the consequences of the incident were as shown in Table 9.2. This might seem that Mary was exhibiting a lot of self-pity and initially she did feel affronted by the head teacher's affirmation of power over her, but the incident did also help her to develop a number of protectors for her future work.

It made her think more about the kind of school she would be happy in, it made her realise that she needed to work in a school that shared her values and beliefs about education. She believed that children needed to be encouraged through praise and celebration of their achievements and she really valued authentic and open relationships with parents. It became clear to her that the school ethos did not match her own as closely as she thought it did. When thinking further about this she realised that there had been numerous other occasions when she had witnessed a harshness towards children that she didn't like and a guardedness towards parents that indicated that parents were seen as inferior to teachers and talked down to. It made her realise that although she needed a job, she needed to look around and not just apply for this job because it was available and because the school expected her to apply. She decided that she would rather do supply work (where she could find out about schools from the inside) until the perfect job came up, rather than find herself somewhere where she lacked autonomy to be herself.

In thinking all the complexity of the situation through, Mary regained her confidence. Everyone said she was an excellent teacher and she knew she was. She had grown as a 'principled professional' and her beliefs in how she used praise as part of her personal pedagogy became a stronger and more important part of her 'principled professionalism'.

Pause to reflect

Think of an occasion in your practice that caused you to ponder the issues where you couldn't stop replaying events in your head. Think about the parties involved and the assumptions that each party might have held. Do you think that analysing such events by looking at assumptions might help you to deal better with them in the future?

Scenario 2: early career teacher

The critical incident

John had a degree in science and had completed a School Direct route to QTS. He had been in his first teaching post for 18 months (the same school where he completed his training) so in total he had been in the school for two and a half years when this incident happened. The school was fairly large for the area, having two classes per year group. The KS1 and KS2 teams seemed to work separately (maybe because five years previously they had been infant and junior schools)

This year John was teaching Year 1 children, whereas his previous experience both in placement and last year had been with older children. He was nervous about taking on Year 1 but had enjoyed the experience so far. He had also been asked to take on an area of responsibility as curriculum lead for science. He was finding the responsibilities of this to be greater than he had imagined and he was told that in order to fulfil his role as science coordinator he needed to observe other colleagues' practice and to produce a coordinator's report (in case we have Ofsted). John felt uncomfortable about this and underprepared for the role. Supply dates had been booked and a schedule arranged for him. On this day he was to observe a Year 2 colleague teaching science. He knew the Year 2 teacher well, she had five years' experience all with Year 2. They had a positive relationship, he had asked her for advice when he found it hard to manage the expectations on him around reading, she had been very supportive and offered her time freely. He found her more approachable that the English coordinator.

On the morning of the observation he felt he was as prepared as he could be. He had read the school's brief observation policy and had clarified with the head the expectations of the report. He arrived at the Year 2 classroom and was greeted warmly by the teacher. He sat down to start his observation. It was clear from the start that the teacher felt that the observation policy was a waste of time and that she treated the whole performativity cycle with some disdain. She was confident with her class, she got good results with the children in her class progressing above expectation in maths and reading. However; she regarded science as something that should be tackled in KS2 and was of little importance at KS1.

The lesson was on keeping healthy and specifically about looking after our teeth. The teacher had a model jaw with removable teeth and set about exploring this with the class. John watched enthusiastically at first. He was in awe of the teacher's ability to enthuse all the children, he felt that he was learning a lot by watching her amazing rapport with even the most behaviourally challenging children. He was so in the flow of the lesson that he almost forgot that his role was to critique the scientific content of the lesson. When he did look closely at the prepared resources he realised that the teacher had named the different teeth in the human jaw incorrectly. He wasn't sure what to do. Should he stop the lesson and correct the teacher? Should he let it pass and deal with it later? But then he felt the children would have learnt facts that were clearly wrong. He made an intuitive decision and decided to interject in front of the class correcting the mistake.

Afterwards the teacher expressed her anger at him for making her look 'a fool in front of her TA and class'. Her attitude towards him was hostile for some time and made him uncomfortable.

When he thought about it John felt aggrieved about the situation. Her scientific knowledge was flawed and she did not hold that science was that important at KS1. This was in conflict with John's own professional identity, shaped through his background as a science graduate and his own beliefs on the importance of the subject. He also felt that children should be taught the correct terminology for scientific concepts from the start, as if they were allowed to continue with the incorrect knowledge this could impact on their future success. They might always wrongly label the teeth for instance. John felt that he had taken the best action in the situation.

Pause to reflect

- If you were John how would you have handled the situation?
- Have you ever been in this kind of situation where whatever you did would potentially have a negative impact one way or another?

Analysing the antecedents and circumstances

The main antecedent here was the Year 2 teacher's lack of scientific expertise.

Analysing the assumptions

Again, in making sense of all the complexity of the situation we have to ana-lyse the assumptions each person makes.

John's assumptions

John assumes that because they have an established relationship, he can interject the lesson without it worrying the Year 2 teacher. He acts intuitively, in the moment, to correct the teacher. He does not consider how his might seem to the children or the TA. John assumes the Year 2 teacher knows how insecure he feels in his role as science coordinator and observer and indeed assumes that she knows that he is in awe of her ability to manage her class.

The Year 2 teacher's assumptions

Mary assumes that John interjected to 'show her up'. She felt that she knew him well and that he abused her trust. She feels that the TA now has diminished respect for her. She suspects that John has moved to Year 1 to 'further his career' and she stereotypically considers him to be a career-driven male who will use his post as science coordinator and Year 1 experi-ence as a stepping stone to deputy headship. She does not see that lesson observation by coordinators helps her to move her practice forward, rather she sees it as a performative tool to allow management to justify their own decision-making on career progression. She has deeply held beliefs about relational practice and values each child's wellbeing above all else. She will challenge colleagues' labelling of children and proactively support the chil-dren who find learning difficult.

In terms of John's critical reflection on the events of the lesson, he feels that the incident has damaged him and his professional identity, as shown in Table 9.3.

Table 9.3 Wellbeing: John

Wellbeing		
Emotional wellbeing (happiness, confidence, lack of stress)	Psychological wellbeing (autonomy, control, resilience, problem-solving skills, attentiveness, connectedness to others)	Social wellbeing (good relationships with others)
John is unhappy because of the change in the Year 2 teacher's behaviour towards him. He feels that she is less friendly and more cautious in her approach to him.	John feels that he had no autonomy in the situation. He was told to observe the Year 2 teacher. The time and lesson were all arranged for him. He was given a brief to follow.	John feels that his social wellbeing has been compromised. He used to ask the Year 2 teacher for support with his own developing pedagogy with regards to reading. He no longer feels that he can approach her for help.
John feels isolated from his colleagues.		John feels a 'frostiness' towards him from the KS1 team. He assumes that they may well have considered his intervention in the lesson to be 'point scoring' on his part.

Through recognising the complexity of the situation, John can use the incident to take action to further his development of 'principled profession-alism'. He decides that he needs to explain his interjection to the Year 2 teacher. It was based on his beliefs about the teaching of science subject knowledge. He can't compromise on those beliefs, but he does acknowledge that he acted intuitively by interjecting because of his principles and that with hindsight he could have chosen another way of indicating the mistake to the teacher without diminishing her authority.

He also recognises that he is underprepared for the leadership role he has taken on and that he needs professional development opportunities to learn about leadership. He further acknowledges his own prioritising of subject knowledge over the relational aspects of teaching Year 1 and decides that is an area he will work on specifically with the more challenging children in his class. Like many teachers, the pressures of performativity have seduced John into believing in the science of deliverology (Pring, 2012). His observation alerted him to the power of the personal.

In both scenarios above, recognising the complexity of the situations can help teachers to move forward and flourish. Often there are policy decisions that mean we cannot have complete autonomy over every situation but

Table 9.4 Flourishing: John

Flourishing				
Personal Enjoyment	Engagement-Flow	Relationships	Meaning	Accomplishment
John is not looking forward to the next observation that he has to carry out.	The incident keeps coming back to him replaying in his mind.	His relationship with the Year 2 teacher has suffered. She is obviously angry and upset.	John is challenging his beliefs about teaching. Previously he had valued subject expertise over teaching style. He now wonders whether ability to form relationships with all members of the class is more important. Should he have left the incorrect knowledge to be corrected later? Should he have had a quiet word with the teacher after the lesson finished?	John feels his accomplishments in attaining the coordinator post are diminished as he feels he lacks the leadership skills to undertake the job effectively.

every teacher has the freedom to develop relational practice according to their principles. Teachers who can critically reflect, analyse assumptions and understand how issues are affecting them, their health and wellbeing stand the best chance of developing resilience and protectors to enable them to flourish in their careers.

References

Brighouse, T. (2006) *Essential Pieces: The Jigsaw of a Successful School.* Available at https://johntomsett.files.wordpress.com/2013/09/timbrighouse-jigsaw.pdf.

Brookfield, S. (1995) *Becoming a Critically Reflective Teacher*. San Francisco: Jossey Bass.

Goodson, I. (2000) The principled professional. *Prospects*, 30(2), 182–188.

Halstead, J.M. (1995) *Values and Values Education in Schools*. Abingdon: Routledge-Falmer.

Lave, J. & Wenger, E. (1997) *Situated Learning: Legitimate Peripheral Participation*. New York: Cambridge University Press.

Noddings, N. (2003) *Happiness and Education*. Cambridge: Cambridge University Press.

Noddings, N. (2006) *Critical Lessons: What Our Schools Should Teach*. Cambridge: Cambridge University Press.

Pacini-Ketchabaw, V. (2015) *Journeys: Reconceptualizing Early Childhood Practices through Pedagogical Narration*. Toronto: University of Toronto Press.

Precey, M. (2015) Teacher stress levels in England 'soaring', data shows. Available at www.bbc.co.uk/news/education-31921457.

Pring, R. (2012) Putting persons back into education. *Oxford Review of Education*, 38(6), 747–760.

Seligman, M. (2012) *Flourish: A Visionary New Understanding of Happiness and Well-Being*. New York: Free Press.

Watson, D., Emery, C. & Bayliss, P. (2012) *Children's Social and Emotional Wellbeing in Schools: A Critical Perspective*. Bristol: Policy Press.

INDEX